Happiness Is

An Introduction To Christian Faith & Life

Alfred E. Mulder

Illustrations by
Wayne De Jonge

Copyright 1968
by the
COMMITTEE ON EDUCATION
of the
CHRISTIAN REFORMED CHURCH
Pocket-Sized Edition, 1975
Second printing, 1976
Third printing, 1978
Fourth printing, 1981
Fifth printing, 1983
Sixth printing, 1984
Seventh printing, 1988
ISBN 0-933140-88-6

All quotations from the Bible are
taken from the King James or Revised
Standard Version.
Used by permission.

Printed in the United States of America

CONTENTS

HAPPINESS IS . . .

Name one person who does not want to be happy and I will name one thousand people who do. Everybody wants to be happy.

What is happiness?

To a small child, happiness may be an ice-cream cone. To a high school sophomore, happiness may be parties and "the group." To an athlete, happiness may be to win. To a young businessman, happiness may be a promotion. To an alcoholic, happiness may be another drink. To a college professor, happiness may be reading a good term paper.

But do these things give real and lasting happiness?

This book explains the meaning of true happiness. Yet it says nothing about ice-cream cones, or parties, or a promotion. The reason is this: true happiness goes much deeper and lasts much longer than any of these things. In fact, when people have true happiness, they keep right on having it—when the ice-cream cones are melted, the parties are over and the promotion doesn't come.

Only the Christian has this true happiness. He is truly happy—or in a state of well-being, as the dictionary defines it—because he has the answers to the deepest needs and problems of life. He is happy with or without all the things mentioned, because he is "in the know" about the basic questions of life, such as who God is, for what purpose He made man and the world, and how we must live to please God and gain eternal life.

This book aims to help you know this true happiness. It seeks to do this by acquainting you with basic facts of the Christian religion. It may not always give the answers you want to hear. Nor does it always give answers that you can understand. It does, however, seek to give honestly the answers of the Bible. By means of careful study of this book, and through a lifelong "courtship" with God's Word, the Bible, you may experience true Christian happiness, too.

CHAPTER 1

A VOICE IN THE DARK

A strange story is told of an ancient Greek philosopher by the name of Diogenes. One night he walked down the streets of Athens, and each time he met someone, he lifted his lantern to study that person's face. When asked why he did this, he replied, "I am looking for an honest man."

This is not a very good way to find out if a man is honest. When it comes to the matter of religion, however, I am sure you will agree that it is almost as difficult to know who is telling the truth as it was for Diogenes to find an honest man. If some American would take his flashlight and shine it in the faces of all the clergymen and other religious teachers to find who was speaking the truth, he could well sympathize with the ancient philosopher. So many voices claim to speak the truth that it is no wonder many people are hopelessly confused.

No matter what religion people hold to, nearly all of them believe in some Power above themselves with whom they must stay on friendly terms in order to be happy. It would be simple if, like Diogenes, we could shine a flashlight into the eye of each religious teacher and find out which one is speaking the truth. But it isn't that easy.

GOD'S VOICE IN THE WORLD

Basically there are two methods by which we can find the truth. One is by looking at the world around us. When you stop to think of it, it is surprising how much the world tells us about religious matters. For one thing, as people throughout the centuries have looked at this great and amazing world, most have concluded that there is a God. They have come up with very different ideas about God, but they are agreed that there is a God of some kind. For another thing, whoever this God is, since He made the world, He must be very great. And if He controls it, He must have tremendous power and wisdom.

It's like John Glenn, our first orbiting astronaut, said when he returned from his history-making flight into space: "Could this world and universe have just happened? Was it an accident that a bunch of flotsam and jetsam suddenly started making orbits of its own accord? I can't believe that. This was a definite plan. This is the one big thing in space that shows me there is a God. Some Power put all this into orbit and keeps it there."

About other things, however, the world does not speak so clearly. To a young married couple deeply in love, God must seem very loving. But to the mother in India, whose starving child is dying, God must seem most heartless and cruel.

So the world tells us some things about which we all agree. If God is God, He must be great, and wise, and powerful. In other things, however, the voice of the world is confusing. How can a good God make possible the happiness of some people and the misery of others? How can God allow the great achievements of man, and at the same time permit man to destroy himself in war? How can the same God allow a gentle rain and a devastating hurricane?

THE VOICE OF THE BIBLE

To straighten out the confusion, and to let people know for sure who is telling the truth, God spoke to us directly. He did this, and continues to do this, in the Holy Bible. The voice of the Bible is to people of every age what a voice in the dark is to a lost pedestrian, telling him where to go and where to turn.

Part of what the Bible tells us we had already figured out. For example, the Bible tells us that "the heavens declare the glory of God" (Ps. 19:1).In this instance the Bible only confirms what the voice of nature already told us. But the Bible also tells us many things we can't figure out from nature alone. The Bible explains, for example, how people first came to be and how they are related to God. The Bible explains how evil came into the world. It explains, too, how it is possible for a good God to be in charge of a world with so much bad in it, and still be a good God. The Bible explains why people must die. It explains that at the bottom of all our problems is the problem of sin.

The fact of the matter is, sin is the reason why the Bible became necessary. If our first parents had obeyed their Maker, there would not be all these unanswered questions. For by not listening to God but choosing sin and unbelief instead, Adam and Eve brought death and all kinds of misery into this world. Thorns and thistles infested the garden. Tornadoes and famine scarred their world. Selfishness and hatred grew like weeds in men's hearts. Furthermore, minds were so damaged by sin, that even when nature spoke clearly of God and His greatness, men still did not understand. This is evident when we observe how people who do not listen to the voice of God in the Bible come

up with different ideas about God and religion. Without the Bible, people are hopelessly confused.

AN INSPIRED VOICE

The Bible is a most remarkable book. Week after week and year after year it makes the list of best sellers. It is remarkable, too, that although the Bible is from two thousand to four thousand years old, it is reliable, trustworthy, and dependable throughout. In fact, with the recent discoveries of ancient manuscripts of the Bible in the Dead Sea scrolls, the accuracy of what the Bible teaches has been verified and our faith in the Bible strengthened. We may add also that by means of what is called "textual criticism" as well as the discoveries of archaeology, the Bible we have now is even closer to the original, and thereby more accurate, than the Bible of a thousand years ago.

What is more, this amazing book of history, poetry, prophecy, and letters, written by many different men under very different circumstances and cultures, and even in different languages, *is one book*. The Bible does not contradict itself. The Bible tells what God has to say for people of every age, today included. "In many and various ways God spoke of old to our fathers by the prophets: but in these last days he has spoken to us by a Son" (Hebrews 1:1). The Bible is also clear. Those who read it prayerfully and carefully can understand what it has to say. Of itself the Bible says in II Timothy 3:16: "All scripture is given by inspiration of God, and is profitable for doctrine, for reproof, for correction, for instruction in righteousness." How the Bible could be such a marvelous book is further explained in II Peter 1:21, when the writer says of the Bible's human authors: "Prophecy came not in old time by the will of man: but holy men of God spake as they were moved by the Holy Ghost."

Why these voices were recorded for us in the Bible is explained by the writer of the fourth Gospel: "These are written that you may believe that Jesus is the Christ, the Son of God, and that believing you may have life in his name" (John 20:31).

QUESTIONS FOR FURTHER STUDY

1. Before man fell into sin, did the Garden of Eden in Genesis 1 and 2 speak more clearly of God than does the world today? See Genesis 3:17, 18; Romans 8:22.
2. What are people able to learn about God from the voice of nature? See Acts 17:23; Romans 1:20-22.
3. Before the Bible was written, how did God speak to people? See for example Genesis 3:9; 18:1, 2; 37:5-11; Exodus 3:1-6.
4. Did God inspire only the Bible, or are there other inspired books in which we can learn about God and His promises? See Galatians 1:8; Hebrews 1:1, 2; Revelation 22:18, 19.
5. In what language was the Old Testament written? In what language was the New Testament written? Do we still have the original manuscripts of the books of the Bible?

CHAPTER 2

BEFORE THE  COUNTDOWN—GOD

We have been living in the space age for some time now. However, the more spectacular space flights still make the news. The most tense moment is the countdown. Ten . . . nine . . . eight . . . seven . . . six . . . . Far more important to the success of the flight, however, is what goes on before the countdown. The millions of tax dollars, the design of the equipment, the accuracy of the scientists, the preparation of the astronauts—these are what make or break the flight. Then, finally, the big moment—five . . . four . . . three . . . two . . . one — LIFT OFF!

Let's make another kind of countdown, down through history. Here, too, the most important part is what comes before. Counting backwards, therefore, 1900 A.D. . . . 1000 A.D. . . . 1000 B.C. . . . 2000 B.C. . . . 8000 B.C. — and at some point beyond which we cannot count: "In the beginning, God . . ." (Genesis 1:1). This is where the Bible makes its lift-off, and begins its flight into time!

GOD INTRODUCES HIMSELF

We notice that the Bible does not argue about whether there is a God. This much God expects us to take for granted. The first verse of the Bible simply tells us that God was always there. The Bible writer sings out to God in Psalm 90:2: "Before the mountains were brought forth, or thou hadst formed the earth and the world, even from everlasting to everlasting, thou art God." Before the world, and before the beginning of the human race, God always was! Furthermore, it seems that almost all people believe there is a God. A recent Gallup poll indicated that 97 percent of those Americans interviewed said they believed in some kind of God.

Who is this God who always was? In the Bible, God never once gives a complete description of Himself; perhaps we would not be able to understand Him even if He did describe Himself fully.

One time, however, God came very close to describing Himself fully. Because of a severe famine, Jacob and his sons (who became the twelve tribes of Israel) left the land of Canaan where they had been living and moved to Egypt in search of food. After living in Egypt for several hundred years, Jacob's descendants grew into a great nation of people. But the time came when God wanted them to leave Egypt and be a separate nation. So God told one of the young Hebrew men, named Moses, to lead His people out of Egypt and back to their homeland. Moses was afraid that the people would not believe him. So he said to God, "Who shall I tell them is sending me?" In answer to his question God said, speaking from a burning bush, "I AM WHO I AM" (Exodus 3:14).

This is God's own description of Himself. In the beginning, God *was*—without need of the sun's light to see, without need of a world to stand on, without need of air to breathe or food to eat, and without need of a mother to give Him birth. And in the present, God *is*—still without need of all those very things that we must have in order to live. So too in the future! God is who He is, and will be who He will be! Incidentally, this is the meaning of the Old Testament name *Jehovah* or *Jahweh*, which is usually translated "Lord."

STRANGE ARITHMETIC

Perhaps both the most interesting and the most mysterious thing about God is the way He describes His *being*. God wants it understood plainly that He is *one* God! It was again through Moses that God told the Jewish people, "Hear, O Israel: The Lord our God is one Lord" (Deuteronomy 6:4). For a God who truly is one being, however, God says some other things that are very strange. When He was busy creating the world He said to Himself, "Let us make man in our image . . ." (Genesis 1:26). Notice: Let *us* make man in *our* image! Some time later, when all people in the world were still speaking the same language, He said to Himself, "Let *us* go down, and there confuse their language" (Genesis 11:7). Again, *us*!

Doesn't God know correct grammar? Doesn't He know that if He is *one*, He ought to say *me* and *my* instead of *us* and *our*? The answer is, as the New Testament makes plain, that the God who is one is also *more than one*! This is why Jesus sometimes caused such excitement. He told His audiences that He and God, His Father, are one (see John 10:31). This is why Jesus commanded the Christian church to baptize new Christians into the name of the Father, and the Son (Jesus), and the Holy Spirit (see Matthew 28:19). Again, of Jesus as "the Word who became flesh" (John 1:14) the Bible says, "In the beginning was the Word, and the Word was with God, and the Word was God" (John 1:1). Jesus demands that He be accepted as God the Son, and *truly* God, just as God His Father is truly God. Peter was right when he said, "You are the Christ, the Son of the living God" (Matthew 16:16). As Jesus also said, "For as the Father has life in himself, so he has granted the Son also to have life in himself" (John 5:26).

This honor that Jesus claims for Himself, He also claims for the Holy Spirit. He told His disciples, "But the Comforter, which is the Holy Ghost, whom the Father will send in my name, He shall teach you all things . . ." (John 14:26). And again, "But when the Comforter is come, whom I will send unto you from the Father, even the Spirit of truth, which preceedeth from the Father, he shall testify of me" (John 15:26). These words came true on the day of Pentecost when the followers of Jesus were filled with the

Holy Spirit (Acts 2:4). The Holy Spirit made His appearance not just as an influence, or a force, or a power. He came to them as a *person*—with a mind (John 14:26), and a will (I Corinthians 12:11), and feelings (Ephesians 4:30). He is God, just as God the Father and God the Son are God. The God who is *one*, therefore, is also *three*!

This is strange arithmetic, no matter how you look at it. However, it does help somewhat to see how the Christian church throughout the centuries has tried to explain this fact about God. The Christian church explains that although there are three *persons* in God, He still is one in *being*. This is where the word "trinity" comes from: tri-unity or three-oneness. God is a "triune" God. Although this term certainly does not take away all the mystery, it does help us to appreciate the wonderful blessing Paul gives to the church in II Corinthians 13:14 when he pronounces the divine benediction: "The grace of the Lord Jesus Christ, and the love of God, and the communion of the Holy Ghost be with you all."

GOD IS MUCH MORE

There are many more things that the Bible tells us about God. The Bible tells us again and again how great and powerful God is (see Psalm 145:3). In fact, so great is He that "ever since the creation of the world his [God's] eternal power and deity has been clearly perceived in the things that have been made" (Romans 1:20). To give some more examples, God is just (see Psalm 145:17), God is holy (see Isaiah 6:3), God knows everything (see Hebrews 4:13), God makes no mistakes (see Job 1:21), God is everywhere (see Psalm 139:8-10), God is kind (see Exodus 34:6), God is a spirit (see John 4:24).

We have yet to mention the best of all for us personally: *God is love!* God proves that He is love by providing the world we live in, the air we breathe, the food we eat, and the people we love. God proves that He is love especially by sending His Son, Jesus Christ, to take away the sin of the world. The Bible says, "He who does not love does not know God; for God is love. In this the love of God was made manifest among us, that God sent his only Son into the World, so that we might live through him" (I John 4:8, 9). When you know the love of God, you know God. And when you know God, you have real happiness.

QUESTIONS FOR FURTHER STUDY

1. Is it possible to understand God fully? See Job 26:14; Psalm 145:3; Isaiah 40:28.
2. How old is the "triune" God? See Genesis 1:2; Psalm 90:2; John 1:1.
3. What does God look like? See Acts 17:29; John 4:24; I Timothy 6:16.
4. Look up the word "pantheism" in the dictionary. Is the doctrine of pantheism any different from saying that God is present everywhere? See Psalm 139:7-10.
5. Matthew 19:26 teaches that God is all powerful. Is this the same as saying God can do anything? What can God not do? See Numbers 23:19.
6. Which characteristic (or attribute) of God shows most clearly in sending Jesus into the world? See John 3:16.

HAPPY BIRTHDAY

"Abracadabra! Ladies and gentlemen, I have just taken this rabbit out of thin air." So says the magician as he holds up the rabbit that he has pulled out of his hat. The children clap their hands, and their parents smile in amusement. But as they smile, they know that the rabbit did not really come from the magician's hat. Rabbits come from rabbits. Nothing really comes from nothing.

Is that always true? Must everything always come from something else? Usually we say *Yes!* You and I came from our parents, and they came from their parents. Monkeys come from other monkeys. Flowers come from flower seeds. Raindrops come from rain clouds.

But what about this big world we are living in? Did this world come from other worlds? What about the great galaxies of stars about us? Did the stars come from other stars? Here we must say *No.* Somewhere there had to be a starting point. Even with people, there had to be the first person. So, too, there had to be the first monkey, and the first flower, and the first raindrop. And, surely, there had to be someone or something beyond this big world and all those millions of stars.

IN THE BEGINNING GOD . . .

Many people believe that some *thing* started it all. They believe that the starting point may have been some unexplained mass of earth, water, and gas. By some strange series of accidents the universe evolved, and so did this earth. From there they suppose (and they can only suppose) that some elementary form of life developed, possibly only a single living cell. Some first *thing*, they say, is the cause of all the other things—apparently some eternal thing.

Of course it is impossible for anybody to prove what actually did happen. No human being was there to watch it take place. The Christian firmly believes, however, that there is a better answer than some eternal *thing*. Although he knows that no human being was there, *Someone* was. God was there at the beginning, for God is eternal. For this reason the Christian is willing to listen to what God has to say about the beginning of things.

The Bible starts out with these words, "In the beginning God created the heavens and the earth" (Gen. 1:1). The starting point is not an eternal *thing*: the starting point is an eternal *God*! Before that first star, there was God. Before that first raindrop and that first ray of light, there was God. Before our first human parents, there was God. God is the creator of them all

How did God do it? To be sure, He has not told us everything. God never intended that the Bible would make geology and astronomy and geography and biology unnecessary. There are other questions that God apparently intended to be left unanswered completely. But there are many questions to which God gave us the answers clearly, in the Bible's account of creation.

AND GOD SAID . . .

Obviously God wanted us to know that He started it all. "In the beginning God created the heavens and the earth." The first matter, out of which God formed the earth and the stars and everything else, was created by God. Webster's dictionary defines "to create" as "to bring into being; to cause to exist." This is exactly what God did. When there was   hing but God only,

God did something that resulted in the existence of the heavens and the earth *in addition to* God Himself. Day after day God said, "Let there be . . . and there was. . . ." We are told in Hebrews 11:3, "Through faith we understand that the worlds were framed by the word of God, so that things which are seen were not made of things which do appear."

The Bible also makes plain that God did this in an *orderly* way. After bringing into being a heaven and earth that at first were "waste and void" (Genesis 1:2), God then went on to give that universe shape and system and sense. The order of creation is related in Genesis 1.

First God separated light and darkness (Genesis 1:3-5). He then gave shape to what the Bible calls "Heaven" (Genesis 1:6-8). This was followed by the forming of the great bodies of water, the earth, and plant life on the earth (Genesis 1:9-13). On the fourth day God set the sun, moon, and stars in their places (Genesis 1:14-19). The next day marked the appearance of life in the air and water: the birds and all kinds of fish (Genesis 1:20-23). The sixth and final day of creation marked God's making of land creatures, including the climax—the birthday of man (Genesis 1:24-27).

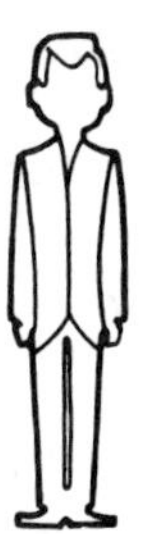

HAPPY BIRTHDAY, MAN!

The birthday of man was a happy birthday because man is the result of God's very special creation. Man is God's masterpiece. Man is the crown of God's entire creative work.

For one thing, God made man in His own image and likeness (Genesis 1:26,27). God gave this man a mind and speech and feelings, such as are found in no other earth creatures. God made this man to think the thoughts of God. God gave this man the ability to do the right and live his life to the praise of his Creator. God made this man to love what God loves. God filled this man with His own "breath of life" and gave him a soul (Genesis 2:7) so that he would live forever.

Another way in which God made man superior to the other living creatures is that God made him a social creature. By a special creative work, God formed a woman from the body of the man (Genesis 2:18-22). The human race is now male and female, but not in the same way as the animals. God created people as male and female "in his own image" (Genesis 1:27). He created people as male and female not merely that they might give birth to more people like themselves, but that they might know marriage (Genesis 2:18, 24). He created people so that they might love one another, and depend upon one another, and talk together, and plan together, and be happy.

HAPPY BIRTHDAY, WORLD!

As a birthday present, God gave those first people that whole big world that He had created. He prepared a garden for them, probably the most naturally beautiful spot in the entire world. "Man and woman," said God, "this is your world. I want you to live from it. I want you to populate it. I want you to rule over it and develop it. It's your world to enjoy!" (See Genesis 1:28-30; 2:20.)

"And God saw every thing that he had made, and behold, it was very good . . . [and] God rested from all his work which he had done in creation" (Genesis 1:31;2:3). As God rested, He must have celebrated. This truly was the happiest birthday ever!

QUESTIONS FOR FURTHER STUDY

1. Why did God create the universe and everything in it? See Psalm 19:1; Romans 11:36.
2. Does the theory of evolution conflict with the biblical account of creation? What is the deciding power in each view? See Hebrews 11:3.
3. How are the words "to create" used in Psalm 51:10; 104:30; Isaiah 45:7?
4. Does the "image of God" in people mean that God and people look alike? See Romans 1:23; I Timothy 6:16.
5. When God first made Adam and Eve, were they "able not to sin"? See Genesis 1:31.
6. What does the fact of common first parents for the entire human race teach us regarding our attitude toward people of races other than our own? See Genesis 5; Acts 17:26; Galatians 3:28.

CHAPTER 4

HAPPINESS LOST

The day on which God created Adam and Eve was a truly happy birthday. And it continued to be happy for some time. The weather and sunshine were always just right. Food was abundant and within easy reach. Adam and Eve enjoyed each other's companionship, and both of them enjoyed the companionship of their God. They loved their Maker; they lived to please Him and were at peace with Him. The world was beautiful, and so was life itself. It was a world of perfect happiness.

A WORLD OF SPIRITS

Besides this beautiful world of stars and planets, of mountains and rivers, of plants and animals and people, God had also created a world of spirits. The Bible calls these spirits *angels*. The angels are pure spiritual creatures (see Ephesians 6:12; Hebrews 1:14), and they have great power. They do not have bodies as we do, and in their spiritual form they cannot be seen by the natural human eye (see Luke 24:39; Colossians 1:16), although they have appeared many times in the form of human bodies. The Bible also tells us that God made thousands of them. Up in heaven where they live with God, they are divided into different classes (see II Samuel 22:11; Isaiah 6:2). There are two angels, in fact, whom we know by name: *Gabriel*, a special messenger of God (see Daniel 8:16; Luke 1:19, 26), and *Michael*, God's warrior angel (see Daniel 10:13, 21; Revelation 12:7).

God created the angels for the same reason He created the rest of the world—for His glory. One way the angels glorify God is by praising Him in heaven (see Psalm 103:20; Revelation 5:11). The other way they bring Him glory is by serving as His helpers in the world, particularly by helping the people God created (see Hebrews 1:14; Psalm 34:7; 91:11, 12; Matthew 18:10; Luke 16:22).

WAR IN HEAVEN

For some reason, which the Bible does not fully explain, a war developed in heaven (Revelation 12:7). The war was started by Satan who became jealous of God. You see, of the thousands of angels God had created, Satan was one of the high-ranking ones in beauty and in power. But he wasn't satisfied with his position. He became proud. God insists, however, that all His creatures remain subject to Him because He alone is God. So when Satan rebelled, God punished him by turning him out of heaven, along with thousands of his followers, called demons (II Peter 2:4). True to their evil natures, they now seek to spoil and ruin what God has made good (I Peter 5:8).

SATAN THE SPOILER

Satan aimed his first "fiery darts" (Ephesians 6:16) at God's happy earth, and particularly at God's creation masterpiece, the man and woman who were made in God's image. He made his approach to the woman through a serpent, one of the most cunning animals God had made (see Genesis 3:1), and at that time probably one of the most beautiful. As a liar and a deceiver by nature (John 8:44), Satan set out to deceive the woman. Little did Eve realize, as she began her fateful conversation with him, what a terrible trap he was leading her into.

This is how the Bible relates the tragic affair. Satan said to the woman, "Did God say, 'You shall not eat of any tree of the garden?' " (Genesis 3:1), The truth was that God had told Adam and Eve they might not eat of one certain tree in the garden. "the tree of the knowledge of good and evil" (Genesis 2:16, 17). God had given this one rule to Adam and Eve as a test of their goodness and their love for Him. He had made them so that they were able to remain good, as He had created them, but God did not want to force them to love Him. He wanted their goodness and their love to be a matter of choice. If they showed their love, therefore, by passing this simple test of obedience, He would reward them with undying happiness. But if they would fail the test, setting their own self-centered interests above the word of God, they would be punished with death (Genesis 2:17).

Eve knew the details of this agreement God had made with them. Not realizing that Satan also knew of this agreement, she pointed out that God had not told them to keep away from *all* the trees, but just one. She also mentioned that if they did not keep away from that tree—the tree of the knowledge of good and evil—the result would be death (see Genesis 3:3).

Satan was quick with his reply: "You will not die. For God knows that when you eat of [that tree] your eyes will be opened, and you will be like God, knowing good and evil" (Genesis 3:4, 5).

Eve didn't quite know what to say, for although most of what Satan said was an outright lie, a little of what he said was true. If they ate of that one tree, they *would* come to know evil as well as good. But the lie she fell for—that they would become like God, and that God was merely threatening them with death to keep them from becoming like Him—*that was utterly false.* It could not have been further from the truth! Adam and Eve would *not* become like God, and Satan knew it. They would only bring God's world and themselves under the curse of death.

PARADISE IS LOST

Then follows that most tragic verse in the Bible, Genesis 3:6, "When the woman saw that the tree was good for food, and that it was pleasant to the eyes, and a tree to be desired to make one wise, she took of the fruit thereof, and did eat, and gave also unto her husband with her; and he did eat."

The happy life in Paradise was over. The arch murderer and liar slunk away in hellish glee. To their sorrow, Adam and Eve found that the forbidden fruit had a bitter effect. The fruit had changed them—but not for the better. Instead of enjoying each other's companionship, they were now ashamed to look at each other, and to be looked at (see Genesis 3:11). Instead of enjoying the companionship of God, they now hid from Him behind the trees God had made (see Genesis 3:8). What a sad picture—trying to hide from the One who knows and sees all! And when God came to them and confronted them with their sin, the picture became even uglier. Adam pointed his finger at Eve. Eve put the blame on Satan. And Satan didn't care!

We wish the story ended here, but it doesn't. The New Testament explains the most tragic consequence of all: "Therefore as sin came into the world through one man and death through sin, and so death spread to all men because all sinned" (Romans 5:12). The agreement God had made with Adam and Eve applied not only to them. It applied to the whole human race whom they represented and who would share the same sinful nature as the first parents. It applied to Adam and Eve's children and their children's children, and their children's children's children. Had our first parents made their choice for God and goodness, they and all their descendants would have reaped the reward of unending happiness. On the other hand, since they freely made their choice for Satan and sin, they and all their descendants now bear the unhappy consequences. The inscription engraved on the tombstone of the entire human race now reads: "All have sinned and come short of the glory of God," and "The wages of sin is death" (Romans 3:23; 6:23). Sin and death have made their entrance into the world. Happiness is lost!

QUESTIONS FOR FURTHER STUDY

1. In what way are angels like God? See Luke 24:39. In what way are angels like us? See Psalm 148:5; Colossians 1:16.
2. What is the work of angels? See Psalm 103:21; Hebrews 1:14. Can you name ways in which angels are greater than man? Can you name ways in which man is greater than the angels?
3. Does Satan still have power to do evil things today? See Matthew 4:1; I Peter 5:8.
4. Were the "evil spirits" of Jesus' time truly the helpers of Satan at work, or was this a mistaken description of mental illness? See Mark 5:1-21; Ephesians 6:12; I John 4:1, 2.
5. Who is to blame for Adam and Eve's failure to obey God—God, Satan, or Adam and Eve themselves? Give reasons for your answer. See Genesis 1:31; 3:6, 12-19.

CHAPTER 5

THE MIRROR LOOKS BACK

A story well-known to many children, and perhaps even more to adults, is the story of "Snow White and the Seven Dwarfs." You may remember that the old queen had the strange habit of talking to her mirror. The mirror, by some unexplained power of knowing all, would talk back to her. One time when Snow White was seven years old, the queen asked as usual:

> "Mirror, mirror, on the wall,
>   Who is fairest of them all?"

To her great unhappiness, the mirror replied very honestly,

> Thou, queen, art fair and beauteous to see,
> But Snow White is fairer far than thee."

We are not surprised that the mirror talked back, because we know this is only a fairy tale. In real life, however, we know that mirrors reflect only what is in front of them. When a girl with lovely blond hair stands in front of a mirror, the mirror reflects the image of a girl with lovely blond hair. When a little boy with spaghetti on his face stands in front of a mirror, the mirror reflects the image of a little boy with spaghetti on his face. That is all a mirror can do. A mirror cannot talk, a mirror cannot look back. It can only reflect what stands in front of it.

NAKED BEFORE GOD

But suppose that a mirror could talk back. Suppose that as you stood in front of it, a mirror could reflect the thoughts of your mind. Suppose that it could look back at you like an X-ray machine, and tell exactly what you are thinking about. Suppose, too, that it had a voice to tell the world what it found out. A rather frightening thought, isn't it?

But this whole idea is not as fantastic as you might think. For if you can imagine a mirror that reflects your thoughts, you will have some idea what it is like to look at yourself as God sees you every moment of your life. The Bible tells us that God knows "the thoughts and intentions of the heart. And before him no creature is hidden, but all are open and laid bare to the eyes of him with whom we have to do" (Hebrews 4:12,13).

How we appear in the mirror of God all depends on what God is looking for. If you can imagine that God wants to see the latest hair styles and particular kinds of clothing, most of us could somehow arrange to look the way He wants us to look. But that isn't what God is looking for. Certainly that is not the way God measures goodness. Something is *good* when it matches up to God's law. For example, since God commands children to obey their parents, children are good children when they obey their parents. In a more general way, all of God's laws for mankind are summed up in this way, "You shall love the Lord your God with all your heart, and with all your soul, and with all your mind. . . . And . . . You shall love your neighbor as yourself" (Matthew 22:37-39). If God sees that kind of love for Him and for one another when He looks into our hearts, then we are good in His sight. We will look good to God only if we look the way God wants us to look.

WHAT GOD SEES

After Adam and Eve fell into sin, they were sent out of the Garden of Eden. Soon children were born to them, and in time there were many people in the world. But when God looked inside these people's hearts, this is what He saw: "The Lord saw that the wickedness of man was great in the earth, and that every imagination of the thoughts of his heart was only evil continually" (Genesis 6:5). Centuries later the picture had not improved one bit. The prophet Jeremiah wrote: "The heart is deceitful above all things, and desperately corrupt; who can understand it?" (17:9). Jesus described the human heart this way: "For out of the heart come evil thoughts, murder, adultery, fornication, theft, false witness, slander" (Matthew 15:19). When we look inside ourselves through the reflection of God's perfect law, that mirror of His law talks back to us: "Evildoer! Deceiver! Corrupter! Murderer! Adulterer! Thief! Liar!" It is true that ". . . through the law comes knowledge of sin" (Romans 3:20). As reflected in the mirror of God's law, and viewed from the inside, man is an ugly sight. Yes, you and I are sinners. We may define sin as anything that goes contrary to God's will and fails to match up to what He requires. Sin is anything contrary to what the law of God demands. When we do what we shouldn't

do, we are guilty of sin. When we don't do what
we should do, this too is sin. And that's us! Some
people prefer to talk about mistakes and errors
and social evils, but the real story of our lives
is much worse than these. We find it told in that
three-letter word: SIN.

AN UGLY DEFECT

Sin is not something that we must learn, as we
must learn how to walk or talk or read. Sin is not
something we pick up by mixing with the
wrong people. We are sinners right from the
start. David says in Psalm 51:5 that we are conceived in sin and born as sinners.

If our sinfulness were nothing more than a lot
of bad habits we picked up somewhere, we
might be able to overcome it. With a little will-
power and some professional help, more than
likely we could get rid of it. But we are born with
sinful hearts. Sin is part of our nature. It can't be
cut out without cutting out our heart. Jeremiah
and Jesus both pointed out that the *heart* of man
is deceitful and wicked. Not the heart that
pumps the blood, but the heart that makes us
think and act the way we do — the inner core of
our personality. That's what is sinful. All the
bad things we do, such as hating and stealing
and gossiping and being selfish, are not like a lot
of scabs on the skin that can be picked off and
healed over. They are like cancer of the liver.
They are like a diseased heart. The fact that we
are sinners means that we are turned against
God from the very center of our being. Sin is a
birth defect, a defect *by nature*.

That explains how Paul can say of himself,
"For the good that I would, I do not: but the evil

which I would not, that I do" (Romans 7:19). It also explains how Paul can say of the entire human race, "All have turned aside, together they have gone wrong; no one does good, not even one. . . . All have sinned and fall short of the glory of God" (Romans 3:12, 23). As Reformed theologians put it, we are "totally depraved." This doesn't mean that we are as bad as we can be. It means, rather, that sin has affected every part of our being. We can't think right thoughts. We can't love as we should. We can't say the right things. We can't work as well as we should, or for the reasons we should. We can't worship as we ought to. We stand condemned in everything we do, "For whatever does not proceed from faith is sin" (Romans 14:23).

Of course, God restrains the evil that is in man. If He did not do so, we could not live on this earth. That is why men are not yet as bad as they can be. To hate someone, for instance, is not as bad as to kill him. And if we work for the wrong reasons, it may be better than not to work at all. We all do a certain amount of natural good because God restrains sin in our lives. But this is not spiritual good — doing good because we love God above all and our neighbor as ourself. And this natural good is not at all able to save us. If God were to let us go, we would immediately fall into far worse sin than we do now. In the condition that we are, we can never save ourselves.

WHY NOT ADMIT IT?

What could be more foolish than refusing to admit that we are sinful? How foolish if we insist on saying, "I'm just as good as the next person." What good does that do? He is a sinner too! Without the help of God, he too is a lost soul. Refusing to admit one's sinfulness is like the reasoning of two men who are dying of cancer: each one refuses to go to the doctor because he is no sicker than the other. The Bible wants us not only to *realize* our sinfulness, but to *admit* and *confess* it — not just to ourselves, not just to our neighbor, but to God! The apostle John tells us in I John 1:8, 9: "If we say that we have no sin, we deceive ourselves, and the truth is not in us. If we confess our sins, he [God] is faithful and just to forgive us our sins, and to cleanse us from all unrighteousness."

To admit and confess that God's law shows you up as a sinner is a hard confession to make — but you'll never be truly happy until you make it.

QUESTIONS FOR FURTHER STUDY

1. The key word in the law of God is _______. See Matthew 22:37-39. What is the real meaning and demand of this word? See I John 4:7-11.
2. How good does God expect people to be? See Matthew 5:48; II Peter 2:15, 16.
3. If we can't be as good as the law of God demands, of what use is the law to us? See Romans 3:20; Galatians 3:24.
4. How does the Bible describe sin? See Isaiah 48:8; Romans 3:10-12; 14:23; I John 3:4.
5. At what age do we become sinful? See Psalm 51:5.
6. Why are people so unwilling to admit that they are sinful? See Jeremiah 17:9; Luke 18:10-14.
7. Can anybody ever be happy if he refuses to admit and confess his sinfulness? Why or why not? See Luke 5:31, 32; I John 1:8, 9.

CHAPTER 6

AN ANGRY GOD

"God is love." So says God's Word in I John 4:8 and in many other places. And so says God's world — in the bright new sun and fresh morning dew, in the graceful swan and the playful chipmunk, in the man and woman made in His image, and in the Garden of Eden that had everything they could ever need. Who else but a God who is love could create a world in which everything was good?

Because God is love, the law for His world is the law of love. The man and woman who were made in His image, and who so fully enjoyed His love, were expected to love Him in return. As a test of their love God asked only that they stay away from one tree, in a world full of trees. But of their own choice, they scorned God's love and refused Him theirs.

So what would the God of love do? Would He look the other way? Would He laugh it off? Would He act as if it had never happened? Is that the way love acts? We know that it does not. When a child disobeys his parents, the parents who laugh it off, or look the other way, are not showing love for their child. Loving parents are justly angry, and they justly punish the child they love. True love is united with justice. Since the love of God is true love, the love of God also is united with justice. And when the love of God is rejected, those who reject it become the objects of His just anger.

THE HIGH PRICE OF SIN

God first pronounced His just anger upon the devil. He cursed the serpent through which the devil spoke, and pronounced the devil's eventual downfall (see Genesis 3:14, 15). Next God declared His just anger upon the man and woman who had so foolishly failed to return His love. Because the woman was the first to reject God's love, she would be ruled by the man (see Genesis 3:16). She was also to know pain, especially in childbirth. The man was punished with the curse of toilsome work. Not just work (this he did even before he sinned), but tiring work — work that would often end in futility (see Genesis 3:17-19). God also pronounced His just anger by placing a curse on the world in which He had placed Adam and Eve. When Adam would plant corn, cockleburs would grow. Where he would plant tomatoes, he would have to hoe out the thorns and thistles that would grow alongside (see Genesis 3:18). Tornadoes, earthquakes, animals turned ferocious — all these came as the result of man's sin and rebellion against God.

The highest price for sin was pronounced last: death! God had warned the man and woman plainly that if they ate of the forbidden tree, they

would die (Genesis 2:17). The awful penalty for rejecting the God of love would be death. Lest we think this too harsh, take the illustration of high-voltage electricity as an example. Electricity is a source of great power and usefulness; but if you violate the basic rules and touch a high-voltage line with your bare hand, you will die. Similarly God's great love is the source of all power and life, but transgress the law of love — and the transgressor must die. So now God told the man: "For out of [the ground] you were taken; you are dust, and to dust you shall return" (Genesis 3:19). The creatures who were created in the image of God, and who were created to live forever, must now prepare to die. Such is the high price of sin.

The punishment for sin has continued its awful march through all the pages of human history. All people are cursed with hatred and jealousy, as demonstrated so early in human history in the story of Cain's murder of his brother (See Genesis 4:1-8). Humanity pays the high price of sin in armed robbery and drug addiction and alcoholism. Humanity pays the high price of sin in poverty and unwanted children and juvenile delinquency and criminal assaults and the bloodshed of war. Humanity pays the high price of sin in disease and suffering. Humanity pays the high price of sin in famines and floods, hurricanes and earthquakes, loneliness and despair, fear and emptiness. Humanity is cursed with sin and the results of sin.

THE GREATEST PUNISHMENT

The greatest punishment of all for human sin is the punishment of separation from God. In the physical world, this is shown most clearly in the curse of physical death. As far as this world goes, how final are the effects of sin when the helpless mother must walk away from the dead body of her little one, or when the aged grandfather places a last kiss on the death-cold lips of his life's partner. Not the prettiest flowers, nor the most expensive caskets, nor the most eloquent sermons can erase sin's awful hurt.

It would be a mistake, however, to suppose that death is only this "return to the dust" that God predicted for Adam and Eve. The Bible describes three kinds of death, and in all three kinds the biggest hurt is that of *separation*. The first kind of death took place on the very day that Adam and Eve sinned. They now were "dead in trespasses and sins" (Ephesians 2:1). Their sins had made a wall between them and God. They were cut off from God's friendship and had become dead toward Him. To live apart from God is death. Adam and Eve now were spiritually dead.

The second kind of death is the death of the body, or the separation of body and soul. Adam experienced this kind of death. This same kind of death comes to each human being in turn — sometimes suddenly, sometimes slowly, but always surely. "Then shall the dust return to the earth as it was; and the spirit shall return unto God who gave it" (Ecclesiastes 12:7). The seed of this kind of death is present from the moment physical life begins. The surest fact of physical life is the awful certainty of physical death.

There is yet another kind of death. You see,

people do not die like dogs. People die like people, with body and soul. For people, therefore, physical death is not the extermination of body and soul, but the separation of the two. So even though the body "returns to the earth as it was," the soul of the unrepentant sinner lives on to face an even greater and more final death. This final death is eternal, the death of hell. The Bible pictures this awful horror in terms of "undying worms" and "unquenchable fire" (Mark 9:48) and "outer darkness and the gnashing of teeth" (Matthew 8:12). What makes this final kind of death so terrible is the fact that the sinner is eternally and permanently separated from God and His love. All this is the high price people pay for their failure to respond in love to the love of their Maker.

PERFECT ANGER AND PERFECT LOVE

In understanding God's anger against sin and His punishment for it, there are two things that must always be kept clearly in mind. The first is this: God's anger is not the result of an imperfect or inadequate love on His part. God's anger is solely the result of man's hatred for God and his enmity toward Him (Romans 8:7, 8). God is angry with men only because they reject His love, and in doing so, reject all that is good and pure and true. They love darkness rather than light.

But — praise the Lord! — there is a second thing God has told us, and that happy fact is this: "The Lord is merciful and gracious, slow to anger, and plenteous in mercy. He will not always chide; neither will he keep his anger for ever" (Psalm 103:8, 9). To prove that this is so, God performed a second work of creation as an expression of His great love: the creation of salvation by Jesus Christ, His Son. Those who receive Jesus Christ as their Savior through faith will be redeemed from sin and death and hell. For by His death as one forsaken by God, Jesus paid the price for all their sins; and by His life of perfect obedience He won for them eternal life. But those who do not accept God's great love offer will finally and eternally know Him as an angry God. Of them it is said: "He who does not obey the Son shall not see life, but the wrath of God rests upon him" (John 3:36).

QUESTIONS FOR FURTHER STUDY

1. Would God be more loving if He did not punish sin? See Hebrews 12:6, 9.
2. Would society be better off if those in authority did not punish wrongdoers? See Romans 13:3. Would society be better off if parents did not punish their children? See Proverbs 13:24.
3. How was the creation itself affected by sin? See Genesis 3:18; Romans 8:19-22.
4. Did God really act upon the warning He gave Adam and Eve in Genesis 2:17? How is death to be understood in this verse?
5. Is it true that the people who suffer most in this life are also the most sinful? See Psalm 73:12; John 9:2, 3; Hebrews 12:3-11.
6. If God is love, how can you explain that He would send anyone to a place so terrible as hell? See Ezekiel 18:23-26; I John 4:7-11.
7. How is the first universal judgment, described in Genesis 6:12-7:24, similar to the last universal judgment, announced in Matthew 24:38-42? What was, and is, the way of escape according to Hebrews 11:7?

CHAPTER 7

GOD HAS A PLAN

Picture before you a federal prison with many hundreds of prisoners. They are here because of the crimes they have committed against society. The floor, the walls, and the ceiling of the prison are made of thick concrete, so that the prisoners cannot escape. Even if they could escape, they would meet with the guns of the prison guards on the outside, and be trailed by their dogs.

BOXED IN BY SIN

The human race is like the prisoners in such a scene. Like the concrete walls of a prison, our sin and God's holy anger against it surround us on all sides. There is no hiding place. There is no escape. We cannot free ourselves from sin or our love for evil. Not even death will free us from our awful predicament, for as we pass over to the life beyond, we will find ourselves face to face with the just Judge against whom we have sinned. There we will have to give account of all that we have ever thought or done or said.

No matter what we human beings do — whether we try to work our way out through good behavior, or whether we try to buy our way out with money and influence, or whether we try to slip away from God unnoticed — nothing will work! We are sinners for life.

God will not contradict His nature by ignoring our sins. And since as sinners we cannot change ourselves or overcome our own sinful will, we can escape our situation only if God Himself should come up with a plan by which we could justly be pardoned and set free.

A PLAN FOR ESCAPE

And God does have such a plan! This is the glad news of salvation. Already in eternity, God planned the salvation of His people, His church. The wisdom of God is such that He knows ahead of time not only what *can* happen, but what *will* happen. The world is not just unwinding on a wild, unpredictable course. God governs and controls all things for His divine purposes. When He placed our first parents in His good world and gave them a free choice for good or evil, in His great wisdom He already knew that they would choose the evil. So, too, as mysterious as this sounds, already in eternity He had a plan by which He would make good to come out of evil. The prophet Isaiah said of God, "I am God, and there is none like me, declaring the end from the beginning and from ancient times the things not yet done . . ." (Isaiah 46:9, 10).

The moving force behind this plan is God's great love for the people He has made. Even though we human beings had revolted against Him, God found "no pleasure in the death of him that dieth" (Ezekiel 18:32). In His great love He provided a way of salvation by which sinners could receive pardon and cleansing, and once more enjoy His love and friendship. As we are told in a most well-known verse of the Bible, "God so loved the world, that he gave his only begotten Son, that whosoever believeth in him should not perish, but have everlasting life" (John 3:16).

THE PLAN UNFOLDS

But why was it necessary for God to send His own Son to save us? Let's look at it this way. If we sinful human beings are going to receive pardon justly, either we will have to pay for our sin ourselves or someone like us — someone who shares our own human nature and can stand in our place — will have to do it for us. Since we can't do it ourselves no matter how hard we try, it will have to be someone else. Moreover, such a one who shares our human nature must be without sin Himself. In order to bear the just punishment of God's wrath against sin, this someone must be able to endure death and yet be strong enough to conquer death and sin and triumph over them. Surely the only person who could do this must be God Himself! The only possibility, therefore, is a Savior who is both God and man.

That is why God sent "his Son, born of woman, born under the law, to redeem those who were under the law, so that we might receive adoption as sons" (Galatians 4:4, 5). What a glorious answer! Our Savior — a *man*, placed in the same category with all of us. Our Savior — *God* Himself, providing the sinlessness and superhuman power necessary to keep all of God's commandments, and pay for the sins of those who could not pay for themselves. As Paul told Timothy, this is God's " . . . own purpose and grace, which was given us in Christ Jesus before the world began" (II Timothy 1:9).

This wonderful plan of salvation — known by God from all eternity — has been unfolded to us gradually in the course of history. In fact, the first announcement of it was made at the very time that Adam and Eve sinned. God told the devil, with Adam and Eve listening in, that the time was coming when "a seed of the woman" would crush his head (Genesis 3:15). That "seed" was our Savior Jesus Christ.

The promise of the coming Savior was repeated and unfolded more clearly as time went on. God called Abraham apart from an evil world and made the promise that through him "shall all the families of the earth be blessed" (Genesis 12:3). To Moses God announced the coming of a great prophet, one like ourselves, who "shall speak unto them all that I shall command him" (Deuteronomy 18:18). Through the animal sacrifices of the Old Testament, God pointed His people forward to some greater "Priest-Savior" who one day would do away with their sins once and for all, and of whom the Old Testament sacrifices were a symbol (see John 1:29; Hebrews 7:27). The plan unfolds in even greater detail through the prophets such as Isaiah, who foretold that "unto us a child is born, unto us a son is given: and the government shall be upon his shoulder: and his name shall be called Wonderful, Counsellor, The mighty God, The Everlasting Father, The Prince of Peace. Of the increase of his government and peace there shall be no end" (Isaiah 9:6, 7).

The New Testament takes up where the Old Testament leaves off, with "the book of the genealogy of Jesus Christ" (Matthew 1:1). It then proceeds to tell us of the fulfillment of God's plan of salvation, as foretold throughout the whole Old Testament. The fourth Gospel first relates the coming of the forerunner or herald of our Lord: "a man sent from God, whose name was John" (John 1:6). Usually he is referred to as John the Baptist. This forerunner or herald "came for a witness, to bear witness of the Light, that all men through him might believe. He was not that Light, but was sent to bear witness of that Light" (John 1:7, 8). Born only six months before Christ, John the Baptist came to be the trail-blazer for the long-awaited Savior. This was the purpose of John's coming as predicted earlier by the prophets.

THE IMPOSSIBLE HAPPENS

"Now the birth of Jesus Christ took place in this way" (Matthew 1:18). As His agent for bringing the "God-man" into the world, God chose a young Hebrew woman by the name of Mary. Mary was a godly woman, a virgin, although she was engaged to be married in the near future. As God told her through an angel, and as He later informed her fiancé in a dream, she was to become pregnant through the mysterious and powerful working of God the Holy Spirit, while she was still a virgin. So by His own mighty power God brought into the world the only possible being who could stand in the place of sinners and still be able to right all the wrong we sinners had done and would continue to do. Very fittingly He was named "Jesus: for he shall save his people from sins" (Matthew 1:21).

The high point of the entire Christmas story is expressed in the message of the angel to the shepherds: "Behold, I bring you good tidings of great joy, which shall be to all people. For unto you is born this day in the city of David a Savior, which is Christ the Lord" (Luke 2:10, 11).

The impossible has happened! The salvation God promised has arrived! The "God-man"

Savior is here, having come "to seek and to save that which was lost" (Luke 19:10). On the night that it happened, not many people took notice of that greatest of all events in the history of our world. But as the familiar Christmas carol says of Bethlehem:

> "Yet in thy dark streets shineth
> The everlasting light;
> The hopes and fears of all the years
> Are met in thee tonight."

QUESTIONS FOR FURTHER STUDY

1. The Bible teaches that God had a plan for the world and history. From the following passages we learn that this plan is *wise, eternal unchangeable, all-inclusive,* and *it works.* Match one or more of these descriptions of God's plan of salvation with each of the following Bible references:

   Psalm 33:11 __________ Luke 12:6, 7 __________
   Psalm 104:24 __________ Isaiah 46:10 __________
   Ephesians 1:4 __________ Acts 2:23 __________

2. If God actually plans and determines the future, does this make Him responsible for sin in the world? See Luke 22:22; Acts 2:23; Romans 1:18-22.

3. Read chapters 1-4 of Matthew's Gospel, listing as many Old Testament quotations as you can find that have to do with the coming and work of Christ.

4. Why did Jesus have to be a man? See Ezekiel 18:20; Romans 8:3; I Corinthians 15:21.

5. Why did Jesus have to be without sin? See Isaiah 53:11; I Peter 3:18.

6. Why did Jesus also have to be true God? See Acts 2:24; II Timothy 1:10.

CHAPTER 8

"MAN OF SORROWS"

"He had no form or comeliness that we should look at him, and no beauty that we should desire him. He was despised and rejected by men; a man of sorrows, and acquainted with grief; and as one from whom men hide their faces he was despised . . . " (Isaiah 53:2, 3). This sounds like the description of some tragic figure: despised, burdened with grief, scarred in body. Whoever He is, how hard He is to look at! And how lonely He must be, for the world has turned away from looking at Him — the world despises Him. He is a "man of sorrows."

When Isaiah wrote these words about seven hundred years before the birth of Christ, he didn't say in so many words that this was Jesus of Nazareth, the coming Savior. But it became evident from the life and teachings of Jesus that this "man of sorrows" of whom Isaiah spoke was none other than the Christ of Galilee.

A HUMBLE BIRTH

Already in the events surrounding His birth, Jesus fits the description. The mother whom God chose for Him was a fine, godly young woman, but humble and unknown. She had no earthly status or prestige. What is more, although she became pregnant through the power of the Holy Spirit, many of her friends and family must have supposed that the baby born to her was an illegitimate child. One of the most cruel blows seemed to strike when she was about to give birth to Jesus. Together with Joseph, now her husband, she had come eighty miles from her home in Nazareth to the little town of Bethlehem, to be enrolled for taxing purposes according to a nationwide decree. Because the hotels and boarding houses were full, she gave birth to the Christ in a stable where animals were sheltered. Talk about humble beginnings!

Of course, for the Son of God even to be *born* as a baby was a humiliating experience. Even if Jesus had been born in a king's palace, or in a stainless steel delivery room of a large city hospital, He still would have lowered Himself a long, long way. Imagine the Creator of heaven and earth becoming a creature! He who is very God laid aside the glory of heaven in order to become man by assuming our human nature (see Philippians 2:6, 7). How great a mystery it is that the Son of God would leave the highest position in heaven as very God (see John 1:1) to assume the lowest place among human creatures — a baby born in a stable and laid to sleep in a manger!

A LONELY LIFE

As far as Jesus' position in the world was concerned, things never did improve for Him. Jesus' stepfather was a carpenter, a trade that made possible only the bare necessities in their home. When Jesus later left His home to enter His public ministry, He had even less of this world's goods. As He told one man who thought he wanted to follow Him: "Foxes have holes, and birds of the air have nests; but the Son of man hath not where to lay his head" (Luke 9:58). In terms of worldly possessions, Jesus was a pauper.

Jesus' ministry lasted about three and one half years — the last three and one half years of His life on earth. It was especially in these final years that the description "man of sorrows" characterized Him. One great sorrow that Jesus endured all through His life was the fact that most people were unwilling to accept Him for who He was — the promised Savior sent of God. When He told the religious leaders that He had existed even before Abraham (since He was God), it made them so angry that they threw stones at Him (see John 10:31). When He performed miracles, He was accused of doing them through the power of the devil (see John 8:48). When He visited the poor, He was labeled a drunkard and a glutton (see Matthew 11:19).

There were those, of course, who accepted Jesus' teaching and believed that He was who He claimed to be. Peter spoke for all the disciples when he said to Jesus, "You are the Christ, the Son of the living God" (Matthew 16:16). However, the attitude of the world as a whole was this: "He was in the world, and the world was made by him, and the world knew him not. He came unto his own, and his own received him not" (John 1:10, 11). As Isaiah had predicted, "He is despised and rejected of men; a man of sorrows, and acquainted with grief . . ." (Isaiah 53:3).

A PAINFUL DEATH

The picture is the ugliest of all in the closing week of Jesus' ministry. On Thursday evening of that week, after He had instituted the Lord's Supper and was in the garden of Gethsemane with some of His disciples, He confessed, "My soul is exceeding sorrowful, even unto death . . ." (Matthew 26:38). The disciples even noticed that " . . .being in an agony he prayed more earnestly: and his sweat was as it were great drops of blood falling down to the ground" (Luke 22:44). But little could they have realized the reason for such agony, much less share it with Him. They did not understand at this point that Jesus was facing a double sorrow: the sorrow that His own people had caused and would cause Him, but most terrible of all the suffering He knew He must bear as the one forsaken by God — as man's sin-bearer.

There was the sorrow caused by Judas' turning traitor, selling Jesus to the enemy for thirty pieces of silver. There was the sorrow caused by the other disciples deserting Him — even Peter (Matthew 26:35, 56). There was the sorrow caused by all the human hatred soon to be expressed toward Him — being spit at, slapped across the face, ridiculed, mocked as He was forced to wear the purple robe and the thorny crown, jeered at by the gawking crowd (see Matthew 26:67; 27:27-44). And there was the sorrow of awful human pain — pain in the knots of the soldiers' whip upon His naked, bleeding back; in the pounding of huge spikes through the flesh of His hands and feet; in the weight of His body upon those wounds; in the agony of physical thirst.

And the deepest, most unspeakable anguish by far, in the closing hours of His greatest grief, was to be forsaken by His Father-God. Hear His agonizing cry as it pierces the darkness of that awful hour: "My God, my God, why hast thou forsaken me?" (Matthew 27:46). His agony and sorrow was His, and His to bear alone! Soon afterward He gave up His spirit, and was buried in a borrowed tomb (see Matthew 27:50-60).

IN MY PLACE

Why was it necessary that one man should suffer so much? There are three possible answers.

The first answer is that of the religious leaders of Jesus' day. Their feeling was, "He asked for it!" They regarded Jesus as an ambitious and evil man. He had tried to tell the world that He was God! The penalty for such "blasphemy" was death of the worst kind (Matthew 26:64, 65).

The second answer is given by many religious leaders today. The sorrows and death of Jesus, they say, show the high price some people must pay for living according to high ideals. Although His death was a tragedy and wasteful, it is an inspiring example to the world.

The third answer is the answer of the Bible: "For our sake he (God) made him (Jesus) to be sin who knew no sin, so that in him we might become the righteousness of God" (II Corinthians 5:21). Jesus died this death for the sake of His own. "For Christ also died for sins once for all, the righteous for the unrighteous that he might bring us to God. . . . He himself bore our sins in his body on the tree" (I Peter 3:18; 2:24).

This third answer, and this answer alone, fits Isaiah's picture of the "man of sorrows." His lack of beauty in the eyes of men, His rejection by the world. His acquaintance with grief — all are explained by Isaiah's further description in 53:4-6: "Surely he hath borne our griefs, and carried our sorrows. . . . But he was wounded for our transgressions, he was bruised for our iniquities: the chastisement of our peace was upon him; and with his stripes we are healed. . . . And the Lord hath laid on him the iniquity of us all."

If you believe in Jesus as the Son of God, and if you regard His sorrows and death on the cross as punishment for *your* sins, then you can write your name in the blank spaces that follow: "He was wounded for _______'s transgressions, he was bruised for _______'s iniquities; the chastisement of _______'s peace was upon him, and with his stripes _______ is healed." When your name belongs in those spaces, you know the deepest meaning of real happiness.

QUESTIONS FOR FURTHER STUDY

1. If someone does not accept the virgin birth as a fact, can he still consistently believe in Jesus as his Savior from sin? See II Corinthians 5:21; Hebrews 4:14.
2. List as many instances of suffering in the life of Jesus as you can think of.
3. In order to be our Savior and overcome our sins, what did Jesus have to do in addition to suffering? See John 4:34; Romans 5:19.
4. Reformed theology describes the suffering and death of Jesus as a "substitutionary atonement." Is this a good term? See II Corinthians 5:21; I Peter 3:18.
5. Would Jesus' suffering have been enough to save us, or did He also have to die? See Genesis 2:17; Romans 6:23; Hebrews 2:9.
6. What does the Bible mean when it tells us to be "crucified with Christ"? See Romans 6:4-7; Galatians 2:20.

THE EASTER PARADE

Every year on Easter Sunday morning, New York City's Fifth Avenue is the scene of an Easter parade. New Yorkers claim this parade to be the outstanding one of its kind. Nevertheless, Easter Sunday morning brings the scene of thousands and thousands of Easter parades. Some of them are in your own neighborhood. They lead to the doors of your churches, and continue down the aisles. The characters in the parades are ladies in colorful new hats and little girls in new dresses. Even if for this one Sunday of the year only, they have put on their Sunday best to join the Easter parade on Easter Sunday. It seems that this is the fashionable thing to do. Besides, so they say, the new clothes are symbols of new life.

THE FIRST EASTER

As unworthy as some people's reasons may be for joining these Easter parades, there is a reminder in these parades of the first Easter Sunday more than nineteen hundred years ago. Granted, that first Easter Sunday did not start

out very happily. After all, less than two days before, Joseph of Arimathea had laid the body of Jesus to rest in his own personal tomb (see Matthew 27:57-60). Since Jesus died a death He did not deserve, the least His friends felt they could do for Him was to give Him a decent burial.

For that reason a group of sorrowing women had started out for the tomb very early on Easter Sunday morning. Their plan was to anoint Jesus' body with the prepared spices they had taken with them (see Mark 16:1, 2). Added to their burden of sorrow was the problem of not knowing how to get at His body. For Jesus' enemies clearly remembered His prediction that He would rise from the dead — even though the disciples themselves had not understood it — and so they had shut off the tomb securely with a huge stone, the governor's seal, and a soldier guard (see Matthew 27:60-66), "... lest his disciples come by night, and steal him away [they said] and say unto the people, He is risen from the dead: so the last error shall be worse than the first" (Matthew 27:64).

What these women discovered when they came to the tomb is what causes Easter to be remembered and celebrated today. The stone was no problem — it had been rolled out of the way by an angel. The soldiers were no problem either — they had fallen to the ground, stunned with fear at the dazzling sight of the angel (see Matthew 28:2-4). Then the angel gave the women joyous news: "Do not be afraid, for I know that you seek Jesus who was crucified. He is not here; for he has risen, as he said" (Matthew 28:5, 6).

With fear and great joy, the women hurried away to tell the glad news to the disciples, even as the angel had directed them. The soldiers also hurried away — but they went to tell the Jewish leaders of the astounding happenings. While the Jewish leaders were frantically making up a story to cover up the facts of the resurrection (see Matthew 28:11-15), the disciples were already running full-speed to the empty tomb, not even daring to hope that what the women had told them was true. First to reach the tomb were Peter and John. Stooping and entering in, they found the grave clothes lying in place — but no Jesus (see John 20:4-9).

The reason was simple, and yet most difficult to believe. Jesus was no longer dead! His body was once again a living body — a gloriously renewed body! If there still were any doubts about this fact, Jesus' friends were soon to be convinced. In this resurrected body Jesus already had appeared to some of the women (Matthew 28:9); first of all to Mary Magdalene as she wept near the tomb (see John 20:14-17), and later to the other women on their way to tell the glad news to the disciples. He also appeared to two of His friends as they walked the road from

Jerusalem to the village of Emmaus, discussing the sad events that had happened (Luke 24:17-31). That same evening He appeared to ten of the eleven disciples as they were gathered behind locked doors. Later He shared fish and bread with them when He met them at the seashore (John 21:9-14). He also showed Himself in Galilee to five hundred Christians at once (I Corinthians 15:6). In fact, it was in the same body that Jesus returned to heaven, and it is in this same body that He now lives and rules with God the Father (Acts 1:9; Ephesians 1:20-22).

A LIVING CHRIST

Paul summed up the facts of the Easter message in I Corinthians 15:3, 4: "For I delivered unto you first of all that which also I received, how that Christ died for our sins according to the Scriptures; and that he was buried, that he rose again the third day according to the Scriptures. . . ." The Christian church desires so earnestly to convince the world of the truth of this message because of the wonderful benefits this glorious happening can have for people *today!* Faith in the resurrection of Christ is the central theme of the Christian message; it is the foundation of Christian happiness.

The first benefit of faith in Christ's resurrection is described in Romans 6:4: "That like as Christ was raised up from the dead by the glory of the Father, even so we also should walk in newness of life." We celebrate the resurrection of Christ not just as a spectacular event that happened years ago. Rather, we celebrate the fact of a *living* Christ who now lives and rules heaven and earth for the benefit of His people and for the glory of God. We celebrate the fact of a living Christ who by His Spirit now lives in the hearts of all who believe in Him. By faith we celebrate *His* resurrection from the dead as a victory over our sin (see Romans 6:11). And by faith in His resurrection we can now begin to live and love and serve as God requires of us (see Romans 7:25).

OUR VICTORY TOO

Newness of life is only the beginning, however. The second benefit of Christ's resurrection is that faith in His victory over death is the guarantee of our victory over death also. When Christ conquered the powers of death and hell by rising from the dead, He shared His victory with all who believe in Him and in His saving power. This is what Jesus meant when He told the sorrowing Martha: "I am the resurrection and the life; he who believes in me, though he die, yet shall he live, and whoever lives and believes in me shall never die" (John 11:25, 26). Just as Jesus died and rose again to undying life, so all who believe in Him have already passed from death into life. Eternal life in the presence of our loving God is already ours, and physical death — through which we must still pass — has become for us the gateway through which we enter heaven's glory (see John 5:24).

The third benefit of Christ's resurrection makes the victory over death complete. It is the hope of His coming again with all the saints in glory. Paul describes that Great Day in these words: "If we believe that Jesus died and rose again, even so them also which sleep in Jesus will God bring with him" (I Thessalonians 4:14). Every believer in Christ ought to be overwhelmed with happiness at this greatest of all hopes, as stated so beautifully by the apostle Paul: "But our commonwealth is in heaven, and from it we await a Savior, the Lord Jesus Christ, who will change our lowly body to be like his glorious body, by the power which enables him even to subject all things to himself" (Philippians 3:20, 21).

No wonder the early Christian church changed the Lord's Day from Saturday to Sunday! Every Sunday is an anniversary of that great life-giving event. And every parade of Christian people to Sunday worship is actually an Easter parade celebrating Christ's resurrection from the dead and the hope of His second coming.

QUESTIONS FOR FURTHER STUDY

1. Should the disciples have known that Jesus would rise from the dead on the third day? See Matthew 16:21; Mark 9:9; John 2:19.
2. Is it possible that Jesus was not really dead when His body was laid in the grave? See Mark 15:44, 45; John 19:32-34.
3. What explanation did the Jewish religious leaders give for the fact that Jesus' body was missing from the grave? See Matthew 28:11-15.
4. For how long a time after His resurrection did Jesus make appearances on earth? See Acts 1:3.
5. Try to list in chronological order the appearances of Jesus following His resurrection. See Matthew 28:9, 16-20; Luke 24:28-39; John 20:18-28; 21:1; I Corinthians 15:5-8.
6. Has the Christian faith any lasting value if we reject the resurrection of Jesus from the dead? See I Corinthians 15:14-19.

MISSING LINKS

The theory of evolution teaches that life has developed from "lower forms." Since no one has ever seen any forms that are between stages—half man and half monkey, for example—they are called "missing links," and the theory of evolution remains a theory.

There are many missing links in life too. Between a new washing machine in the store window and the help it gives to a busy housewife, there is the missing link of money to buy it. A sack of lawn seed and rich, green lawn are "linked" together by planting, watering, fertilizing, and mowing.

In somewhat the same way, there are missing links between the salvation God has created and our personal enjoyment of it. Salvation was made by the loving plan of God the Father and by the birth, death, and resurrection of God the Son. But this salvation is not personally received or enjoyed until God the Holy Spirit provides the missing links that He alone can provide: a new life in the heart of the sinner, followed by repentance for sin and faith in the saving work of God.

BORN OF THE SPIRIT

The first missing link in our salvation is brought out in a conversation between Jesus and Nicodemus. Jesus told Nicodemus that "unless one is born anew, he cannot see the kingdom of God" (John 3:3). As Nicodemus wondered how a grown-up person possibly could be born a second time, Jesus explained that He was talking about a being "born anew" in the sense of getting new *spiritual* life from the Holy Spirit. In other words, getting a new heart. Jesus' own words are, "Truly, truly, I say to you, unless one is born of water and the Spirit, he cannot enter the kingdom of God" (John 3:5). Another name for this being "born of the Spirit" is *regeneration*.

When a person is "born of the Spirit" he becomes a different person on the inside. The Holy Spirit performs a "heart transplant" in a spiritual sense. For the Holy Spirit takes the human heart, which by nature is "hostile to God" (Romans 8:7), and gives a new heart that loves God instead of fighting against Him. The person "born of the Spirit" becomes willing to listen to God, learn from Him, and live for Him (see I Corinthians 2:6-16). Paul was talking about regenerated people when he said: "And you he made alive, when you were dead through the trespasses and sins in which you once walked, following the course of this world . . ." (Ephesians 2:1, 2).

TELL GOD YOU'RE SORRY

When the Holy Spirit provides for the first missing link of a new and "open" heart, the second missing link comes into the picture—*repentance*. When the Holy Spirit was "poured out" on the Christian church on Pentecost Sunday, the apostle Peter told his audience to "repent . . . for the forgiveness of your sin; and you shall receive the gift of the Holy Spirit" (Acts 2:38). Paul preached basically the same sermon to his audience at Athens: "[God] commands all men everywhere to repent" (Acts 17:30). This also was the plain message in the Old Testament, as we read in Ezekiel 33:11: "As I live, says the Lord God, I have no pleasure in the death of the wicked; but that the wicked turn from his way and live."

The person who is "born of the Spirit" is sorry for his sins. He is sorry that he keeps on sinning in his thinking, doing, and speaking. And he tells God so. Like the prodigal son who went humbly and repentantly back to his father after having wasted his life, the born-again Christian gets down on his knees before his Maker and confesses: "Father, I have sinned against heaven and before you; I am no longer worthy to be called your son" (Luke 15:21). Furthermore, he seeks to prove his prayerful confession of repentance with a life of repentance. In the power of the Holy Spirit, who now lives in his heart, he does his best to "put off [the] old nature which belongs to [the] former manner of life . . . and put on the new nature, created after the likeness of God . . ." (Ephesians 4:22, 24).

FAITH THAT SAVES

The third link needed to connect the salvation God created to our enjoyment of it is *faith*. The Bible says that "without faith it is impossible to please him. For whoever would draw near to God must believe that he exists, and that he rewards those who seek him" (Hebrews 11:6).

Missing link, you say? Who doesn't believe that God exists? If you would ask people you meet on the street if they believe that God exists, nine out of ten would say *Yes* without even giving the matter a second thought. Faith in God seems to be the rule rather than the exception. So why do we say that faith is a *missing* link?

The answer is simple and sad. Not all people who "believe that he exists" have the kind of faith that links them to salvation. The devils have faith that God exists, but it certainly is not the kind of faith that will save them (see Matthew 8:29; James 2:19). There are many people who believe there is a God, and yet will not enjoy salvation because their faith is of the wrong kind (see Matthew 7:21).

For one thing, faith that saves must be based on *knowledge*. This is obvious. "How shall they believe in him of whom they have not heard?" the Bible asks in Romans 10:14. Of all the people who claim to have faith in God, the larger part of them have never really met God or know what He stands for. Faith that saves, on the other hand, is grounded in a knowledge of the Bible and what it says about God. Faith that saves includes the knowledge of ourselves as lost sinners, the knowledge of Jesus Christ who came to earn forgiveness for sins, and knowledge of the kind of life God expects of those who have found forgiveness. As Paul said, "So then faith comes by hearing, and hearing by the word of God" (Romans 10:17). There is no Christian faith without a knowledge of the Christian gospel.

Second, faith that saves includes *trust* that God will do for us what He has promised. This is what makes the difference between the faith of devils and the faith of Christians. Christians know not only that there is sin in the world and that Jesus Christ died on the cross to take away sin. Besides that, Christians trust that the saving work of Christ was for their sins.

Faith that saves, therefore, is much more than having an idea that somehow and somewhere there is some kind of God. Faith that saves consists of very personal trust in the God who can be known from the Bible. Faith that saves is both a *knowing* and a *trusting* faith in the God of the Bible. And this kind of faith links together the salvation God made and the Christian who enjoys that salvation.

Praise God the Father who planned salvation! Bow in repentance and faith before God the Son who earned it! Give thanks to God the Holy Spirit, who by giving new life, enables people to enjoy it!

QUESTIONS FOR FURTHER STUDY

1. Is the Holy Spirit a person or a power, a "He" or an "It"? See Matthew 28:19; John 14:26; Ephesians 4:30.
2. When did the Holy Spirit come to the Christian church? See Acts 2:1. How many days was this after Christ ascended to heaven? Did the Holy Spirit exist before this time? See Genesis 1:2; Psalm 104:30; II Peter 1:21.
3. Should a person know when the Holy Spirit has regenerated him? If so, how can he be sure? See John 3:8; Romans 8:16; Galatians 5:25.
4. What different kinds of faith are pictured in the parable of the sower? See Matthew 13:18-23.
5. Why do some people who hear the gospel have saving faith, while others with the same opportunity do not have it? Acts 16:14; Romans 9:16; II Thessalonians 2:9-12.
6. Does the Holy Spirit ever bring people to repentance and saving faith without the hearing of the Christian message? See Romans 10:14, 17.

CHAPTER 11

A LASTING FRIENDSHIP

Friendship is based upon faith. A beautiful example of this is the friendship that was born the day young David killed the Philistine giant with his slingshot. At that time David the shepherd boy and Jonathan the prince became the best of friends. The Bible says that "the soul of Jonathan was knit with the soul of David, and Jonathan loved him as his own soul" (I Samuel 18:1). At first this friendship was based upon only a *knowing* faith in each other. Their friendship grew into a lasting friendship, however, as their knowing faith in one another led to a deep *trusting* faith in one another. In spite of the hatred of Saul, Jonathan's father, for David,

David so trusted Jonathan as to place his very life in Jonathan's keeping (see I Samuel 19, 20).

The example of David and Jonathan teaches us something about the friendship that exists between a Christian and his God. That friendship, too, is based on faith—the Christian's faith in God. What is more, Christian faith includes those same two elements: knowing faith and trusting faith—knowledge of God and His promises, and a trustful placing of one's very life in God's care and keeping.

JUSTIFIED BY FAITH

The reason that friendship with God is based on faith is found in what faith does. Paul explains what faith does in Romans 5:1: "Therefore, being justified by faith we have peace with God through our Lord Jesus Christ." Faith justifies a person before God because it is the means by which Christ's saving work is applied to us. Justification is a courtroom term. Today we use the terms "acquittal" or "not guilty" to express the same thought. The idea is that a person who is justified by faith in Christ is no longer at war with God, or God with him. The Christian and his God are at peace with one another. They are friends.

How a Christian is justified can be pictured in terms of a courtroom scene. Every person who ever lived stands before God as a guilty criminal before a judge. We are sinners: therefore we must plead guilty (see Romans 3:10-21).

Furthermore, since God is a just God, there is only one possible verdict: "The wages of sin is death" (Romans 6:23). Before the sentence is pronounced, however, and before God assigns anyone to the eternal death of hell, each person is given opportunity to defend himself. The person who is not a Christian has nothing to say. But as the apostle John said of Christians, "If any man sin, we have an advocate with the Father, Jesus Christ the righteous" (I John 2:1). Christ takes sides with the Christian as his "advocate" or lawyer. And the case that Christ presents in defense of the Christian is air tight.

The Bible makes clear that the sentence of death is removed by faith in "Jesus Christ the righteous." You see, when Jesus suffered and died on the cross, He did so to pay the penalty for human sin (see John 1:29; Galatians 1:4; Hebrews 9:28; I Peter 2:24). Therefore, in defense of anyone who has answered the call to faith in Christ and His penalty-paying work, Christ bases His case on the fact that this person's sentence *has already been paid!* The Christian has nothing more to pay, since Christ has already paid his debt on the cross. As Paul told the Galatian Christians, "Christ hath redeemed us from the curse of the law, being made a curse for us" (Galatians 3:13).

Standing on the record of *our* life and deeds, the only possible verdict God can give us is "Guilty!" But when we stand before God by faith in Jesus Christ, the only possible verdict is, "Not guilty!" God accepts the innocence and righteousness of His Son in our defense, as though it were our very own (see II Corinthians 5:21).

It is for this reason that the Bible makes the call to faith so plain and strong. You must "believe on the Lord Jesus Christ, and you will be saved, you and your household'' (Acts 16:31). Again, ''And this is his commandment, that we should believe on the name of his Son Jesus Christ . . .'' (I John 3:23). As the apostle John said toward the close of his Gospel, ''But these are written that you may believe that Jesus is the Christ, the Son of God, and that believing you may have life in his name'' (John 20:31).

A LASTING FRIENDSHIP

But who is to say that this friendship with God will be a lasting friendship? If I am a Christian now, is there any reason to believe that I still will be a Christian next year, or two years from now, or when I die? Let's answer that question by asking another question: Why do you have faith today? You have faith because the Holy Spirit gave you a new life and made you want to believe. As Lydia ''gave heed'' because ''the Lord opened her heart'' (Acts 16:14), so it is with everyone who has faith. ''By grace you have been saved through faith; and this is not your own doing, it is the gift of God'' (Ephesians 2:8).

It is true that when we do have faith, we are responsible for that faith. We must take care of it and make it grow stronger.

Nevertheless, faith is not our own achievement to begin with. The Christian has faith only because God has given it to him. And since friendship with God rests upon faith that only God can give, that friendship with God can be lost only if God takes it away. The Bible assures us, however, that God will not do that. Jesus said of His sheep, ''I give them eternal life, and they shall never perish, and no one shall snatch them out of my hand. My Father, who has given them to me, is greater than all, and no one is able to snatch them out of the Father's hand" (John 10:28, 29). The Christian can be sure "that neither death, nor life, nor angels, nor principalities, nor powers, nor things present, nor things to come, nor height, nor depth, nor any other creature, shall be able to separate us from the love of God which is in Christ Jesus our Lord" (Romans 8:38, 39).

A DAILY FRIENDSHIP

The lasting nature of friendship with God becomes even more wonderful when you realize that you don't have to wait until you die to enjoy it. The Christian can be sure of that friendship all along the way, since "by God's power [we] are guarded through faith for a salvation ready to be revealed in the last time" (I Peter 1:5). Friendship with God is a daily pleasure. Jesus once said, "Are not two sparrows sold for a penny? And not one of them will fall to the ground without your Father's will. . . . Fear not, therefore; you are of more value than many sparrows" (Matthew 10:29, 31).

A poet caught the beautiful lesson of Jesus' words in these verses

    "Said the Robin to the Sparrow,
      'I should really like to know
      Why these anxious human beings
      Rush about and worry so.'

> "Said the Sparrow to the Robin,
>   'Friend, I think that it must be
>   That they have no heavenly Father,
>   Such as cares for you and me.' "

If you are a friend of God by faith in Jesus Christ, you have all the reason in the world to be different from all "anxious human beings." For as friends of God "we know that all things work together for good to them that love God, to them who are the called according to his purpose" (Romans 8:28). Friendship with God is a lasting friendship that brings great happiness.

QUESTIONS FOR FURTHER STUDY

1. What was the theme of the great Protestant Reformation? See Romans 1:17 (KJV); Galatians 2:16. How did this theme differ from the teachings of the Roman Catholic Church of that day?
2. In justification by faith the judge is _______, the accused is _______, and the defense attorney is _______.
3. How were people who lived before the time of Christ justified? See Romans 5:1; Hebrews 11:13.
4. Is justification by faith a work of God, a work of man, or a work of both? See Ephesians 2:1, 8, and give reasons for your answer.
5. The Christian's assurance of God's daily care is called *providence*. Are sorrow and sickness included in this providence of God? See Job 1:21; Romans 8:28; Hebrews 12:6.
6. Tell in your own words how the story of Joseph recorded in Genesis 37-47 is a shining illustration of the providence of God. What texts especially show that Joseph recognized this?

CHAPTER 12

WHEN YOU ARE DEAD

A little boy once wrote a letter to God that read something like this: "Dear God, I'd like to know what it is like to be dead. I don't want to be dead. I would just like to know. Signed, Bobby." As brief as the letter is, it runs over with childish honesty. But it is not a childish question he asks of God. It is a question that a lot of people are asking, and a question to which everyone would like an answer.

Doctors tell us that it usually isn't too hard to die. One doctor wrote, "Most people die in painless peace because they are physically benumbed. . . . The patient suffers little near the end." Another doctor said, "Death is usually preceded by a willingness to die. I have never seen it otherwise. It is always easy at last." But there are other things we know, too. The dead body soon turns cold and stiff. In time it will begin to decay; and given enough time, it will turn into dust. Even if death comes easy at the end, and no matter how "nice" the body may look in the casket, death is ugly.

This is not an answer to Bobby's question, however. It tells us only what happens to *other* people when they die, at least as far as we can see. Bobby wanted to know what it would be like for *him* to be dead. This is the question we want answered too: What will it be like for *me* when I am dead? What will it be like for *you*?

A BODY AND SOUL

We are so much concerned with this question because the Bible teaches clearly that for people there *is* a life after death. It may appear, of course, as though there is no difference between the death of animals and the death of people. But this is not so. When a dog dies, he is dead — period! However, when people die, they do not die like dogs. They are not made like dogs in the first place. God made people with a body and a soul, or a body and a spirit (see Matthew 10:28; Romans 8:10). So even after you have spoken your last word and breathed your last breath, and lie "moldering in the grave," *you live on.* Your spirit or soul keeps right on living. As the Bible says in Ecclesiastes 12:7: "Then shall the dust return to the earth as it was: and the spirit shall return unto God who gave it."

We can understand why this happens when we understand the reason for death. When God breathed into that first human being "the breath of life" (Genesis 2:7), He intended that man should live forever. Death came into the picture only after our first parents had sinned. "Sin came into the world through one man and death through sin, and so death spread to all men because all men sinned" (Romans 5:12). Death is necessary as the fulfillment of God's threatened penalty for sin.

For the person who has not found forgiveness in Christ, death is the greatest human tragedy possible. For him, not only does death separate the body from the soul. Death eternally separates the soul from God (see Chapter 6 on hell).

WHEN A CHRISTIAN IS DEAD

For the Christian, however, death is by no means a tragedy. True, the Christian still undergoes the separation of body and soul, and separation from his loved ones on earth (we can't escape the results of sin completely). But when the Bible talks about death for the Christian, it

talks about it in expectant terms. To those who have Christ as their Savior, "Death is swallowed up in victory" (I Corinthians 15:54).

For the Christian, the first thing that happens at death is that the soul goes up to heaven. The Bible knows nothing of a "purgatory" or "sleeping soul" as the first stage of life after death. The "spirit returns to God who gave it" *immediately*. As Jesus told the converted thief on the day that he died, "Today shalt thou be with me in paradise" (Luke 23:43). The day of the funeral, then, is no time to pray that the dead person's soul may go to heaven to be with God. If he died as a Christian, his soul went to join the Lord the very moment that he died.

FOREVER WITH THE LORD

From then on the soul "shall always be with the Lord" (I Thessalonians 4:17). What such a life is like, human language is not able to describe. The Bible says that "no eye has seen, nor ear heard, nor the heart of man conceived what God has prepared for those who love him" (I Corinthians 2:9). The best way we can be given a glimpse of such a wonderful place as heaven is by the use of comparisons. This the Bible does when it tells us that heaven is something like a great palace or mansion (see John 14:2). It is something like a marvelous, "out-of-this-world" city, decorated with all the riches of the earth (Revelation 21:10-26). It is something like an oasis in the desert (Revelation 22:1, 2). But the greatest glory of heaven is the presence of God (Revelation 21:1-3).

It is no wonder that human language and understanding limit us in trying to understand what life is like in such a place. The Bible tells us that life in heaven will be very different. While it is apparent that some of the joys of life on earth will not be a part of life in heaven, the fact is that the joys of heaven will so far outweigh the passing joys of earth that there will no longer be need for them.

In the center of life in heaven will be the presence of our gracious God, a fact too marvelous to be fully understood or appreciated by us who are still sinners. The best news about heaven is this: "Behold, the dwelling of God is with men. He will dwell with them, and they shall be his people, and God himself shall be with them; he will wipe away every tear from their eyes, and death shall be no more, neither shall there be mourning nor crying nor pain anymore, for the former things have passed away" (Revelation 21:3-5). Because heaven is where God is, there cannot possibly be any hint of sadness there, or pain, or sin. It is a place of unending and glorious perfection.

With such a wonderful future ahead, the Christian can go through life and death with this courageous and hopeful attitude: "We are of good courage, and we would rather be away from the body and at home with the Lord" (II Corinthians 5:8). Bernard of Cluny, who lived about eight hundred years ago, glimpsed something of the glory of heaven when he wrote in the song, "Jerusalem the Golden":

> "I know not, O I know not
> What joys await us there,
> What radiancy of glory,
> What bliss beyond compare!"

QUESTIONS FOR FURTHER STUDY

1. Christ died and rose again to overcome death for all Christians. See I Corinthians 15:57; II Timothy 1:10. How then do we explain the fact that Christians still must die? See John 11:25, 26; Romans 5:12; 6:23.
2. May a Christian ever pray for death? May a Christian ever want heaven so badly as to take his own life? See Exodus 20:13; I Kings 19:4-7; Philippians 1:23.
3. Will some Christians have greater glory in heaven than other Christians? See Matthew 25:14-30; I Corinthians 3:13-15; II Corinthians 9:6.
4. The Roman Catholic teaching about purgatory gives the idea that we on earth can help those who have already entered the next life to advance in glory and happiness. Discuss this teaching in the light of Luke 16:26; II Corinthians 6:2; II Peter 2:9.
5. What are some things Christians will be doing in heaven? See Revelation 5:9-14; 7:9-17.
6. Psalm 23 is often read or recited at funerals. What verses in this Psalm are especially helpful in facing grief or death? If you do not already know this Psalm, be sure to memorize it.

CHAPTER 13

THE FINAL REENTRY

There was dancing on the streets of Moscow that day of April 12, 1961. Russia had just opened the door to a new age. A little before 9:00 A.M. that morning, from somewhere in the Soviet Union, a five-ton space vehicle lifted off its launching pad and soared into space. For 89 minutes it whipped along at a speed of 17,000 miles per hour in a path about 200 miles above the earth. Even more spectacular was the fact that in the spacecraft rode a young Russian — Yuri Gagarin — and upon reentering the earth's atmosphere and making a safe landing, he stepped out *alive!*

THE "LIFT OFF" AT JERUSALEM

Many Russians would be surprised to learn that Gagarin was not the first space traveler. An earlier flight took place nearly two thousand years ago on a little hill outside Jerusalem. It was quite different, to be sure, from the flight Gagarin made. There was no launching pad, there were no booster rockets, there was not even a space vehicle. Just a small gathering of Jesus and His friends, some clouds in the sky — and suddenly a Man in space! The Bible says: "And when he [Jesus] had spoken these things, while they [the disciples] beheld, he was taken up; and a cloud received him out of their sight" (Acts 1:9).

On this day that Jesus ascended, He was "made to sit at [God's] right hand in the heavenly places" (Ephesians 1:20). The angels and other powers of heaven are answerable to Him (see Ephesians 1:20-21; I Peter 3:22). He holds the steering wheel to the universe (Matthew 28:18; Ephesians 1:21,22). He is the head and leader of the Christian church (Ephesians 1:22; 5;23). He presents to the Father the prayers of the Father's children (John 15:16; Hebrews 4:14-16). And He promises to have heaven ready for Christians when they get there (see John 14:2). Unlike that Russian space traveler who went along only for the ride, Jesus ascended into heaven to take control of heaven and earth.

THE PROMISE OF REENTRY

A space flight is not completed until the astronaut has made reentry and has returned to this planet Earth. The same is true with the ascension of Christ. As His disciples watched Him "lift off" and disappear behind a cloud, an angel said to them: "Men of Galilee, why do you stand looking into heaven? This Jesus, who was taken up from you into heaven, will come in the same way as you saw him go into heaven" (Acts 1:11). Jesus will make reentry! He will return! He made this promise even before He left: "And if I go and prepare a place for you, I will come again, and receive you unto myself; that where I am, there you may be also" (John 14:3). Paul repeats this promise many times, in words such as those of I Thessalonians 4:16: "For the Lord himself shall descend from heaven with a shout, with the voice of the archangel, and with the trump of God."

What a day that will be! It will be remembered as the day of a worldwide resurrection. "Do not marvel at this," Jesus said, "for the hour is coming when all who are in the tombs will hear [my] voice and come forth, those who have done good, to the resurrection of life, and those who have done evil, to the resurrection of judgment" (John 5:28, 29). Everybody is going to be there! Your childhood playmates, your grandparents and other relatives, people from the East and from the West, both great and small, both kings and paupers — all men, even from the beginning of time. "When the Son of man shall come in his glory, and all the holy angels with him, then he will sit upon the throne of his glory: and before him shall be gathered all the nations . . ." (Matthew 25:31, 32).

THE DAY OF JUDGMENT

The day of Christ's return will also be remembered as the great Day of Judgment. When He first came to earth, Christ came to save. When He comes a second time, it will be to judge. John writes regarding the vision he received: "And I saw the dead, small and great, stand before God; and the books were opened: and another book was opened, which is the book of life: and the dead were judged out of those things which were written in the books, according to their works" (Revelation 20:12). Each and every person who has ever lived will be publicly judged "according to what he has done in the body" (II Corinthians 5:10).

This judgment according to works in no way overlooks the fact that only those who have a knowing and trusting faith in Jesus as their Savior will be saved (see Chapters 10 and 11). In the judgment, too, it will be evident that "by grace you have been saved through faith; and this is not your own doing, it is the gift of God" (Ephesians 2:8). The fact that God will judge according to what we have done simply underlines that "faith by itself, if it has no works, is dead" (James 2:17). If our faith in Christ is real, our lives are going to show it. Understand clearly, then, that when "God shall judge the secrets of men by Christ Jesus" (Romans 2:16), "he will render to every man according to his works .... There will be tribulation and distress for every human being who does evil ... but glory and honor and peace for every one who does good" (Romans 2:6, 9, 10).

THE TIME OF REENTRY

The Bible does not say when Christ's final reentry will take place. Jesus told His disciples, "It is not for you to know times or seasons which the Father has fixed by his own authority" (Acts 1:7). We do know, however, that His second coming will be sudden (I Thessalonians 5:2), and at a time when many people will least ex-

pect it (Matthew 25:1-13; I Thessalonians 5:2, 3). We also know that certain things must happen before Jesus will return. Jesus will not return until the "gospel of the kingdom will be preached throughout the whole world, as a testimony to all nations" (Matthew 24:14). He will not return until after the world has seen many "false Christs" and "false prophets" (Matthew 24:5, 11; I John 4:1-3) and the church has experienced a great loss in membership (Matthew 24:10, 24; II Thessalonians 2:9-11). Before Christ returns, the world will also see a "man of lawlessness"(II Thessalonians 2:3-9; I John 2:18; Revelation 20:3). This man, known also as "antichrist," will make one last great effort at breaking up the Christian church.

When these "signs" (Matthew 24:3) come about — and it will take careful watching to recognize them — then the final reentry of the ruling Christ is near. "Then shall appear the sign of the Son of man in heaven" (Matthew 24:30).

WATCH THEREFORE

Whether this great day takes place tomorrow or a thousand years from tomorrow should make no difference in the way we live. Whether we first meet the Lord in death or at His coming, there will then be no more time for getting ready. "Behold, now is the day of salvation" (II Corinthians 6:2). Peter's advice applies equally in either case: "Therefore, beloved, since you wait for these [things], be zealous to be found by him without spot or blemish, and at peace" (II Peter 3:14). Jesus said it most clearly: "Watch therefore, for you know neither the day nor the hour" (Matthew 25:13).

To every true child of God, the final reentry of Christ will be a glorious and happy sight. For "just as it is appointed for men to die once, and after that comes judgment, so Christ, having been offered once to bear the sins of many, will appear a second time, not to deal with sin but to save those who are eagerly waiting for him" (Hebrews 9:27, 28). "Amen. Come, Lord Jesus!" (Revelation 22:20).

QUESTIONS FOR FURTHER STUDY

1. How many days after Easter is Ascension Day? See Acts 1:3.
2. What does it mean that Jesus is at the "right hand" of God? See Ephesians 1:20, 21; Colossians 3:1.
3. What will happen to the world at the time of Jesus' return? See Matthew 24:29, 35; I Peter 3:10-13.
4. Will we be judged for *everything* we have ever done or said or thought? See Matthew 12:36; Romans 2:16.
5. Discuss the relationship between faith and good works as it is set forth in Ephesians 2:10; I Thessalonians 5:8-11; James 2:14-26; II Peter 1:10, 11.
6. When Christ returns, will Christians be caught by surprise? See I Thessalonians 5:1-5.

CHAPTER 14

UNDER NEW MANAGEMENT

Perhaps you know some ambitious young man who has bought a run-down business place and is attempting to make a go of it. He puts a new front on the store, remodels the interior, and stocks up with a new line of merchandise. Then as a final plea to the neighborhood to buy his goods, he decorates the front window with a large sign in bold red letters: "Under New Management." This sign tells people that this store isn't what it used to be. It may be at the same old location, and may sell the same basic product. But it is a new store, offering better service and new satisfaction. Someone new is managing it now.

This is similar to what happens in the life experience of the Christian. In this story the young businessman is a symbol of God. The place of business stands for the Christian. The Christian, before he becomes a Christian, is broken down, worn-out, and doomed for bankruptcy. But when God buys him out and works him over, the service he then performs and the satisfaction his life brings truly merit the sign: "Under New Management." He is now under God's management.

HEADED FOR DISASTER

As we learned in detail in Chapters 4 and 5, any person whose life has not been changed by the saving power of God is in a lost and sinful condition. That person may be in an obviously sinful condition such as an alcoholic, a criminal, a wife-beater, a drug addict, or a prostitute. Or he may appear to be in rather good condition, such as mayor of a city, a loved and respected man. He may be the family doctor or the friendly grocer. But if Jesus Christ does not live in his heart by faith, his life is headed for eternal disaster.

Anyone who is not yet living by faith in God is living primarily for himself. And anyone who is living for himself is headed for trouble. The Bible says, in fact, that "whatever does not proceed from faith is sin" (Romans 14:23). So even those people who seem to be dedicating their lives to the service of humanity and the improvement of the world, unless they do so for God's sake, are working for a losing cause. We are partners in a thriving business only when "whether you eat, or drink, or whatsoever you do, do all to the glory of God" (I Corinthians 10:31). Our lives will show a profit only when God is the manager.

WHEN GOD IS MANAGER

When God does truly manage our lives, there are bound to be some striking changes. One change will be in our attitudes and outlook on life. The despair and emptiness and disorderliness will be gone. For when we live under God's management, it's no longer a matter of helplessly taking things "the way the ball bounces." We now can travel the rough roads as well as the smooth ones with a quiet and peaceful trust in our Father's leading (see Psalm 37:3-7).

For another thing, life with God as the manager is much less complicated. We don't have to break our heads trying to lay out our own future. Whether we are gaining friends or losing them, whether we are getting rich or spending our last dime, we know that God is still in control of our lives. So we need only follow the rules for living that He has set down in the Bible. As long as our lives are patterned after His will, we are assured that we are part of a winning venture (see Matthew 6:25-34).

A third and most surprising benefit is that when we look to God to manage our lives, we are happier! The lonely housewife doesn't have to look to some other man for happiness, because the home that is under God's management is a happy home. The Christian businessman doesn't have to make his margin of profit from dishonesty, because he has discovered that a business built on honesty and integrity is a more enjoyable business. Whether we are at work — whatever our work may be — or whether we are simply relaxing among friends, life is more truly happy and satisfying when we live it in God's presence. Those who have committed their lives to Him can say with the Psalmist, "The Lord is my shepherd; I shall not want" (Psalm 23:1).

MAKING A U-TURN

A most convincing example of these truths is Paul, who became the Christian church's first foreign missionary. Paul was a Roman citizen, a fact that entitled him to many rights and privileges that other people did not have. Besides, he was a Pharisee (Pharisees were the religious leaders of their day), and came from a family of Pharisees. He had a good education and enjoyed a position of respect among his neighbors. Before his conversion, he made the claim that if anybody wanted to talk about being religious, he could match the best of them (see Philippians 3:4-7). He was so devoted to his religion that he gladly would see dead all those who taught or believed anything else. He was, in fact, the cause of the death of many Christians. But life was a nightmare for Paul, because he was fighting against God.

One day God stopped him along the road and caused him to make a "U-turn." God turned him around spiritually (see Acts 9:1-20). We call this experience *conversion*. From that day on, the direction of Paul's life was turned around. The old Paul died, and a new Paul took his place (see Ephesians 2:1, 2; 4:22-24). The persecutor of Christians turned into a preacher of Christ.

This new way of life seemed much harder at times, for Paul lost the respect and prestige he once enjoyed. But now he had something far more worthwhile: the peace that comes from following the will of God. No matter how rough things got — and they did get pretty rough once in a while (see II Corinthians 4:8-11) — Paul stuck with it, willing to "prove what is that good, and acceptable, and perfect will of God"

(Romans 12:2). The whole difference was that Paul was "under new management."

THANK YOU, LORD

A similar change must take place in the life of anyone who becomes a Christian. All Christians must make this "U-turn" from death to life, and from a life of sin to a life for God.

But what accounts for this drastic change in direction?

The basic reason is that *God has changed them*. Of course, God doesn't lead Christians around on a leash. He doesn't force them to go to church, and to pray, and to witness to others about Him. Because they have a new heart, they want to do these things!

This change of behavior is the Christian's willing thanksgiving to God for the great salvation He has given. Christians are thankful to God for what He has done for them. Recall from the illustration at the beginning of this chapter that God rescued the Christian from bankruptcy. God is not forced to do this either. God only wanted to do this because He loves us. For this same reason the Christian now willingly and gladly cooperates in whatever the Lord asks of him.

You see, God is not just the Christian's new manager. God is the Christian's Savior! Paul summed it up when he said, "O wretched man that I am! Who shall deliver me from the body of this death? I thank God through Jesus Christ our Lord" (Romans 7:24, 25). A new and better life, therefore, is the Christian's way of saying:

"Thank you, Lord, for saving my soul.
    Thank you, Lord, for making me whole.
    Thank you, Lord, for giving to me
    Thy great salvation, so rich and free."

QUESTIONS FOR FURTHER STUDY

1. Since we are saved only "by grace through faith," does the kind of life that we live really make any difference? See James 2:26.
2. There is a "negative" change and a "positive" change in the conversion of a Christian. See Romans 6:11; Ephesians 2:1, 2; 4:22-24; and explain what these "negative" and "positive" changes are.
3. Paul's conversion was very sudden. Are all true conversions sudden? See II Timothy 3:14, 15.
4. What requirements must be met in order for anything we do, say, or think to meet God's approval? See I Samuel 15:22; Romans 14:23; I Corinthians 10:31.
5. When a person becomes a Christian, does this change his whole life? Does he lose interest in earthly things, such as cars, clothes, food, sports, and social life? See Matthew 6:24; Romans 12:2; I Corinthians 10:31.
6. What guidelines are given us to follow in living the Christian life? See Psalm 119:11; Philippians 2:5; I Peter 2:21.

CHAPTER 15

MY GOD AND I

Perhaps you have heard the song:

> "My God and I go in the field together,
>   We walk and talk as good friends should
>   and do,
>   We clasp our hands, our voices ring with
>   laughter,
>   My God and I walk through the
>   meadow's hue."

God is a Spirit (see John 4:24), and since spirits have no hands or feet (see Luke 24:39), it is not really possible physically to walk and talk and laugh with God. But the idea that fellowship with God is possible certainly is true. The Christian enjoys the things that God enjoys; he shares the same loves with God, the same hates; he shares with Him the same goals and ambitions. In other words, the Christian is happy because he lives according to God's laws for human behavior.

Jesus summed up all of God's laws when He said: "You shall love the Lord your God with all your heart, and with all your soul, and with all your mind. This is the first and great commandment. And a second is like it, You shall love your neighbor as yourself" (Matthew 22:37-39). As plain and simple as Jesus puts it, we with our sinful minds are not able to understand and apply the law of love as we should. We need the help of the Ten Commandments, which explain in more detail what it means to love God and our neighbor.

THE TEN COMMANDMENTS

The giving of the Ten Commandments is one of the high points in the entire Old Testament. For two days before God gave these commandments to Israel, the people "consecrated themselves," and on the third day God Himself spoke from heaven with ". . . thunders and lightnings . . . and the voice of the trumpet exceeding loud so that all the people who were in the camp trembled" (Exodus 19:16). After these preparations God gave them the Ten Commandments as they are recorded in Exodus 20:1-17.

These Ten Commandments were by no means the only laws God gave to Israel. He gave them laws for religious ceremonies, care of the poor, marriage, government of the Jewish nation, and many more. Many of these laws were given only to the Jews as a nation, and many others have been fulfilled with the coming of Christ. But the Ten Commandments—also called the "moral law" — still stand as binding for Christians of all ages because these laws express God's character.

NO OTHER GODS

The first table of the law includes commandments one through four and deals strictly with our relationship to God. In the first commandment God tells us: "I am the Lord thy God, which have brought thee out of the land of Egypt, out of the house of bondage. Thou shalt have no other gods before me'' (Exodus 20:2, 3). God is very exclusive in the love He demands of us. As a husband demands the exclusive love of his wife, so God demands that we love Him first and foremost. He wants to be worshiped as the *only* God because He alone is God; He alone is the source of all love and righteousness. God objects to our worshiping any other person or object than Himself — whether that be a savings account, a new car, a good job, or a person whom we love. For we may not worship the creature more than the Creator (Romans 1:25). God doesn't want to play second fiddle. Not even the laws of parents and governments may stand in the way of obedience to our Creator — God (see Acts 5:29). As Jesus reminded the devil in Matthew 4:10: "Thou shalt worship the Lord thy God, and him only shalt thou serve." Commandment one demands that God be number one!

IN SPIRIT AND TRUTH

The next three commandments in the first table of the law tell us how we must place God first in our lives. Commandment one tells us whom to worship; commandment two tells us how to worship. In our worship of God, "Thou shalt not make unto thee any graven image, or any likeness of any thing that is in heaven above, or that is in the earth beneath, or that is in the water under the earth: thou shalt not bow down thyself to them, nor serve them: for I the Lord thy God am a jealous God . . .'' (Exodus 20:4, 5). God is not shaped like a mountain, or a sacred cow, or a human-looking statue, and He doesn't want to be worshiped through means such as these. See Deuteronomy 4:15; Acts 17:29; Romans 1:23.

Jesus stated clearly the kind of worship God wants when He said in John 4:24: "God is a Spirit: and they that worship him must worship him in spirit and in truth." Where we gather for worship and with whom we gather for worship are not nearly so important as the thoughts and feelings of our hearts. Our worship may be expressed in various ways: songs, prayers, meditation, offerings, the reading and explaining of the Bible. Furthermore, it may be formal or informal, traditional or modern, planned or spontaneous. But whatever it is, it must be in keeping with the truth of God's Word, and it must be sincere. Acceptable worship is an honest and personal communing between God and His people.

MY GOD'S NAME

It seems strange that commandment three is even necessary. It is unthinkable that friends of God would toss His name around carelessly, or worse still, use it as a swear word. Yet the use of God's name "in vain" is one of the most common sins in the world today. Almost anywhere you go, men and women of all kinds — and sometimes even children — use the names of God again and again as if God were a *nothing!* A missionary in New York City once said that some children do not even know that "Jesus

Christ" is not a swear word.

Such senseless use of the names of God, whether by swearing or mockery or simple carelessness, is sin! God hates it, and in commandment three He forbids us to use His name in such vain and blasphemous ways. "Thou shalt not take the name of the Lord thy God in vain; for the Lord will not hold him guiltless that taketh his name in vain" (Exodus 20:7). Jesus expressed this commandment in these words: "Let what you say be simply 'Yes' or 'No'; anything more than this comes from evil" (Matthew 5:37).

Living with God is a daily privilege. Sunday through Saturday the Christian enjoys friendship with God. In commandment four, however, God requires that one day out of every week be set aside: "Remember the sabbath day, to keep it holy. Six days shalt thou labor, and do all thy work: but the seventh day is the sabbath of the Lord thy God; in it thou shalt not do any work . . . for in six days the Lord made heaven and earth, the sea, and all that in them is, and rested the seventh day: wherefore the Lord blessed the sabbath day, and hallowed it" (Exodus 20:8-11).

God was thinking of our needs when He commanded that every seventh day should be ". . . a holy sabbath of solemn rest to the Lord . . ." (Exodus 35:2). Many times it has happened that people who "burned the candle at both ends" day in and day out, without regard for God's day of rest, suffered for it later. One doctor said that most rest periods he orders his patients are only "Sundays in arrears."

But God also was thinking of our relationship to Him. If our friendship with God is to remain alive and happy, it must have constant care. Therefore the Bible warns sternly against

". . . neglecting the assembling of ourselves together, as the manner of some is, but exhorting one another . . ." (Hebrews 10:25). Also, both the example of Jesus, who "as his custom was, went into the synagogue on the sabbath day" (Luke 4:16), and the example of the early church, which ". . . continued steadfastly in the apostles' doctrine and fellowship, and in breaking of bread, and in prayers" (Acts 2:42), underline the importance of Sunday worship, regular Bible study, Christian fellowship, and prayer as absolutely necessary to healthy Christian faith and happy Christian living.

QUESTIONS FOR FURTHER STUDY

1. Who or what may be "god" to an atheist? a Communist? a playboy? a businessman? a housewife?
2. In what way is God a "jealous" God? In human relationships, is jealousy always bad, or is it sometimes honorable? Does the same hold true in God's relationship to us? If so, why? See Exodus 20:5; Jeremiah 14:22.
3. May a Christian "swear to tell the truth" in court? See Matthew 5:33-37; Romans 1:9; Hebrews 6:16.
4. In the Old Testament the people of God celebrated the "sabbath" on Saturday. Christians now observe the "Lord's Day" on Sunday. Why has the Christian church made this change from the seventh to the first day? See John 20:11, 19; I Corinthians 16:2.
5. How can a Christian decide what he may or may not do on the Lord's Day? See Matthew 12:12; Romans 14:13-15.
6. What does the fourth commandment say about the other six days? See Exodus 20:9.

CHAPTER 16

A HAPPY HOME 

In the early spring of 1863, during the American Civil War, the Union and Confederate armies were camped across from each other along the Rappahannock River near Fredericksburg — the Union army on the northern bank of the river, and the Confederate army on the southern bank. As the fighting would let up toward evening, the soldiers of both armies would play and sing some of their favorite songs. On the Union side the band would play songs like "The Battle Hymn of the Republic"; then the Union soldiers would shout and cheer. On the southern side the band would play "Dixie," followed by a great cheer from the Confederate army. One evening the Union army band played "Home, Sweet Home"; and when it finished playing, *both* sides cheered. "Home, Sweet Home" thrilled the hearts of both Union and Confederate soldiers.

What makes home so special is the fact that people are social creatures. People want to share their lives with other people. People want to love and be loved. At first Adam was the only human being in the world. Although he was kept very busy tilling the ground, keeping the Garden of Eden (Genesis 2:15), and naming the animals (Genesis 2:19, 20), God knew that the companionship of animals was not enough. "Then the Lord God said, 'It is not good that the man should be alone; I will make him a helper fit for him' " (Genesis 2:18). The Genesis story then tells how ". . . the rib which the Lord God had taken from the man He made into a woman and brought her to the man" (Genesis 2:22).

Now there were people on the earth — a man and a woman. This marked the beginning of society. And since God created these first two people as "male and female" (Genesis 1:27), the beginning of society also marked the beginning of marriage and a happy home.

TWO BECOME ONE

The marriage union is a sexual union. In marriage a man and a woman, each with a different body, are drawn together. God so created man and woman that in the act of sexual intercourse, which is the privilege of marriage, "they become one flesh" in the fullest sense of the term (Genesis 2:24). The world's first husband said of the world's first wife, "This is now bone of my bones, and flesh of my flesh: she shall be called Woman, because she was taken out of Man" (Genesis 2:23). The creation story continues,

"Therefore shall a man leave his father and mother, and shall cleave unto his wife: and they shall be one flesh" (Genesis 2:24).

It is also by means of this sexual union that one important reason for marriage is fulfilled — that of continuing the human race by the birth of children. God explained this already to that first couple in the Garden of Eden, "Be fruitful, and multiply, and replenish the earth, and subdue it . . ." (Genesis 1:28).

Were the marriage union no more than a sexual union, however, it could exist in a parked car, or on a blanket at the beach, or in a backstreet boarding house, or in a laboratory. The beauty of the marriage union is that in true marriage the union also is spiritual. Husbands and wives share not just their bodies. They share their homes, their money, their relatives, their joys, their sorrows, their interests, their secrets, their ambitions. The apostle Paul compares the marriage union to the kind of union that exists between Christians and their Christ (see Ephesians 5:21-33). In Christian marriage, the husband and wife are united not just in "flesh"; they become united in spirit. And this kind of union fulfills the second God-intended purpose of marriage — the happiness of those who marry.

NO TRESPASSING

When sin came into the world, however, it took away some of the original beauty of marriage. Already in Genesis 3, the woman betrayed the husband, and the husband accused the wife (see verses 6 and 12). This was only the beginning of a long history of marriage misery that seems to have reached an all-time high in the twentieth century. Therefore, in order that marriage in a sinful world might bring even some of the happiness God intended it to bring, He gives some very definite rules to follow.

The marriage union must be *exclusive!* Commandment seven says, "Thou shalt not commit adultery" (Exodus 20:14). No unmarried couple is allowed the privilege of sexual intercourse, no matter how much they love each other, and no matter what their intentions are. This privilege is reserved for marriage! Furthermore, marriage unites a man and a woman to one another only and exclusively! The marriage union allows no vacations, no exchanges, and no trespassing. And breaking of this rule is labeled by God: *adultery.* So serious is the sin of adultery that Jesus listed it (and it alone) as a just ground for divorce (Matthew 5:31, 32). With this one exception, God demands that the marriage union continue "as long as you both shall live." Paul says: "Thus a married woman is bound by law to her husband as long as he lives" (Romans 7:2). And what applies to the wife also applies to the husband.

AN UNEQUAL PARTNERSHIP

God also established a very definite order for the husband and wife in marriage. The common notion that marriage is a fifty-fifty proposition does not agree with the clear teaching of the Bible. Marriage is a partnership, but it is not a partnership in the sense that the duties of the husband and the wife toward each other are identical. The man is the head of the woman in marriage right from the beginning, as Paul explains in I Corinthians 11:8-10. Paul teaches the same thing in Ephesians 5:22, 24: "Wives, submit yourselves unto your own husbands, as unto the Lord. As the church is subject unto Christ, so let the wives be to their own husbands in every thing.'' (Also see Colossians 1:18; Titus 2:5; I Peter 3:1, 2.)

No husband may jump to the conclusion, however, that he is the "big chief" and that his wife's entire world must center around him. Actually, his duties toward his wife are greater. The law for the husband is the example of Christ Himself: "Husbands, love your wives, as Christ loved the church and gave himself for her. Even so husbands should love their wives as their own bodies. He who loves his wife loves himself. For no man ever hates his own flesh, but nourishes and cherishes it . . ." (Ephesians 5:25, 28, 29). The Christian husband loves his wife devotedly and expresses that love by providing for her needs where possible, by treating her with respect and honor, and by living to make her happy. True love, after all, is not the kind that takes but gives (see Ephesians 5:25; I John 4:9, 10).

A THIRD PARTY

Another requirement for a happy home is that both parties in the marriage union be Christian. The Bible says, "Do not be mismated with unbelievers. For what partnership have righteousness and iniquity? Or what fellowship has light with darkness? What accord has Christ with Belial? Or what has a believer in common with an unbeliever?" (II Corinthians 6:14, 15). A religiously mixed marriage is a mismatch in the deepest sense. Only when the husband and the wife share Christ, can they truly share each other, spiritually as well as sexually. The promise of a lasting and happy marriage is the greatest when God is the third party. An unknown poet has said,

> "I've never known divorce to break a home
> Where a man and a woman pray.
> They are closest to God and each other
> Who kneel at the close of each day.
> I've never known disaster to crush
> A home with great burdens to bear,
> Where a husband and wife, amid this earth's strife
> Make use of the power called prayer."

QUESTIONS FOR FURTHER STUDY

1. Discuss birth control in the light of parental responsibility, the health and welfare of parents and children, and the population explosion of the twentieth century.
2. Jesus teaches that adultery justifies divorce. Does adultery demand divorce, or can it be forgiven by God? by the party who is sinned against? See Matthew 18:21, 22; Mark 12:31; John 8:11.
3. Does the Bible ever give grounds for "separation"? See I Corinthians 7:10, 11.
4. Homosexuality is abnormal to say the least. Is it an illness? a sin? or both? See Romans 1:26, 27; I Corinthians 6:9.
5. Is it possible to break commandment seven without engaging in sexual intercourse? See Matthew 5:28.
6. Why is the proper control or expression of sex so important? See I Corinthians 6:19, 20.
7. Read Paul's hymn of love, I Corinthians 13. Underline the words that hold especially good advice for husbands and wives.

TO LIVE IS TO LOVE

Perhaps no word in the English language is more written about, read about, sung about, and talked about than the word "love." At the same time, perhaps no word in the English language is more misunderstood, misused, and abused.

What is love? Is it nothing more than what we read about in the paperbacks, or hear about in the weekly hit tunes? Is it really love that a teen-age girl feels for the team hero? Is it love that drives a family man to the arms of another woman? Can even the pride and pleasure that parents have for their children always be called true love?

Not necessarily! A person who loves only for

what he or she gets out of it does not know the true meaning of love. True love is not the same as self-seeking or selfishness, nor even the same as having pride in someone. True love does not express itself in taking, but in *giving!* True love is not self-seeking, but *self-sharing!* (See I Corinthians 13:4, 5.)

TO LOVE IS TO GIVE

The perfect example of love is God Himself. The Bible says: "God is love. In this the love of God was made manifest among us, that God sent his only Son into the world, so that we might live through him" (I John 4:8, 9). God proved His love, not by taking from us, but by giving to us that most expensive gift of all — His Son — and through His Son giving happiness and eternal life.

God demands that we show the same kind of love toward one another that He has shown toward us. The apostle John tells us, "Beloved, if God so loved us, we also ought to love one another" (I John 4:11). As God loved, we must love. As God gave, we must give. "By this we know love, that he laid down his life for us; and we ought to lay down our lives for the brethren" (I John 3:16). This is what God is telling us to do in the last six of the Ten Commandments.

A COMMANDMENT WITH A PROMISE

Learning this kind of love must start early in life. "Honor thy father and thy mother, that thy days may be long upon the land which the Lord thy God giveth thee" (Exodus 20:12). God did not give parents to us simply to clothe our backs, feed our mouths, and fill our pockets with spending money. God gave us parents that we might honor them, obey them, and live for them in love!

Making or breaking this fifth commandment has far-reaching consequences. If we never learn to give respectful and obedient love to our parents, then neither are we likely to give such love to our teachers, our employers, or our government officials. And there is little argument that most delinquency, crime, and disrespect for law and authority point back to lack of respect for authority and lack of love in the home.

This, too, is where the promise of this commandment fits in. When children learn respectful and obedient love in the home, those children and that nation have the promise "that it may be well with [them] and that [they] may live long on the earth" (Ephesians 6:3).

WHAT LOVE DOES NOT ALLOW

"Thou shalt not kill" (Exodus 20:13). A parent who beats his child to death does not love him. A robber who shoots the cashier does not love him. The driver who fails to regard his high-powered automobile as a potential killer does not show love to those who get in his way. The doctor who does not seriously try to preserve and repair the lives of his patients fails to love them.

In fact, "anyone who hates his brother is a murderer" (I John 3:15), for hate is a contradiction of love. Hate is the desire to destroy. It is the desire to take instead of to give. And not only does love for life forbid our destroying it, or wanting to destroy it, love for life demands that we do our very best to preserve it and improve and develop it — both our lives and the lives of others.

The same principle applies in commandment seven: "Thou shalt not commit adultery" (Exodus 20:14). Many people argue that the sex act is permissible before or outside of marriage, as long as it is done in love and as long as neither one of the parties "gets hurt." The Bible teaches, however, that you cannot commit adultery in love. Adultery is a contradiction of love because adultery is selfish. Adultery is taking instead of giving. True giving and sharing in sex is possible only within Christian marriage.

Christian love also forbids lying. Commandment nine reads: "Thou shalt not bear false witness against thy neighbor" (Exodus 20:16). If we love people, it makes no sense that we should tell lies about them. To destroy a person's reputation through lies, rather than showing love, takes from him one of his most precious possessions. As Proverbs 22:1 tells us, "A good name is to be chosen rather than great riches . . ." Sometimes, of course, love for others may demand that we respect the truth, speak it only with the greatest gentleness and tact. The basic principle, however, is that love expresses itself in truth. "Therefore, putting away falsehood, let everyone speak the truth with his neighbor, for we are members one of another" (Ephesians 4:25).

God says in commandment eight: "Thou shalt not steal" (Exodus 20:15). Christian love does not allow stealing because Christian love is primarily giving, and stealing is taking what does not belong to us. Love demands honesty — as an employee in doing the work you are getting paid to do, as an employer in paying for the work you get done, as a customer in paying for the goods received, and as a businessman in delivering the goods for which you have been paid. Christian love demands honesty in the school assignment on which you write your name, and with the income tax report to which you attach your signature. If you truly "love your neighbor as yourself" (Matthew 22:39), you will not take credit for something that is not yours. At the same time, love demands that you take full responsibility for what is yours — for better or for worse!

Closely related to this is the tenth commandment: "Thou shalt not covet . . . anything that is thy neighbor's" (Exodus 20:17). Instead of coveting, we must learn to be content with what God has given us. And in our contentment we even must learn to be happy about the possible greater happiness of others. You see, we *love* them!

WHAT'S MINE IS YOURS

A beautiful story of love in action is told by Jesus in Luke 10:30-37. Briefly, a man was walking along the road when some hoodlums attacked him, robbed him, and beat him half to death. As he lay along the road, both a priest and a Levite passed by, looked at him, and walked on. Later a Samaritan — one of a "lower class" of people in the eyes of the Jews — came by and helped him.

This story describes three basic attitudes toward life, which someone has summed up this way. The hoodlums' attitude was, "What's yours is mine; I'll take it." They coveted, they stole, and they nearly killed. The attitude of the priest and the Levite was, "What's mine is mine; I'll keep it." Their sin is that they failed to love. Only the "Good Samaritan" understood that to live is to love, and to love is to give. His attitude was, "What's mine is yours; I'll share it." Jesus then concluded the story by saying, "Go and do likewise."

The Bible says, "Owe no one anything, except to love one another; for he who loves his neighbor has fulfilled the law. Love does no wrong to a neighbor; Therefore love is the fulfilling of the law" (Romans 13:8, 10). In every aspect of daily living, to live happily is to love.

QUESTIONS FOR FURTHER STUDY

1. Can occasions arise when love for God makes it impossible for Christians to obey parents or others in authority over them? See Acts 4:19; Romans 13:1.
2. Is mercy-killing ever an act of love? Discuss this question in the light of commandment six.
3. Evaluate smoking, alcoholism, and drug addiction in the light of commandment six. Also see I Corinthians 6:19, 20; 10:31.
4. Read the story of David and Bathsheba in II Samuel 11:2-27. What three commandments did David break? What particular warning do you find in this story?
5. In the light of Genesis 3:4-6; Proverbs 26:20, 22; Ephesians 4:25; James 1:26; and Peter 4:8, how would you evaluate unkind truth? gossip? false insinuations? white lies? flattery? outright lying?
6. Does being content mean that we are not to be ambitious and seek advancement? To what extent may Christians be concerned about "keeping up with the Joneses"? See Matthew 6:25, 33; I Corinthians 10:31; II Thessalonians 3:6-13.

CHAPTER 18

THE BREATH OF LIFE

When God made the first man from the dust of the ground, He "breathed into his nostrils the breath of life; and man became a living soul" (Genesis 2:7). What God did to make Adam alive we cannot understand. But we do know that for people to stay alive, they must breathe.

The new life of the Christian is kept alive through breathing also. For the Christian, the breath of life is prayer. James Montgomery wrote,

> "Prayer is the Christian's vital breath,
> The Christian's native air. . . . "

For a Christian to survive without prayer is as unthinkable as for a human being to live without oxygen. Prayer is the lifeline between God and the Christian.

THE ART OF PRAYER

Sometimes we get the idea that praying is a hard thing to do. Perhaps you know someone who has been a Christian for years, and yet freezes up at the thought of leading a group — or even members of his own family — in prayer. Perhaps you yourself feel that you can't pray "good enough." Even Jesus' disciples once said, "Lord, teach us to pray" (Luke 11:1). Usually, however, the difficulty is not so much in talking to God, which prayer really is, but in talking to God in a way in which we think other people will approve.

Jesus made clear in His many lessons on prayer that what others think doesn't really matter. In fact, He severely criticized people who insist on using the right kind of words. "And in praying do not heap up empty phrases as the Gentiles do; for they think that they will be heard for their many words. Do not be like them . . ." (Matthew 6:7, 8). God understands *You* as well as *Thee*, and *has* as well as *hast*. God understands incorrect grammar. God simply wants you to talk to Him, in language that you yourself understand and feel.

Prayer posture is not that important either. Usually we are taught to pray with our eyes closed and hands folded, or even to get down on our knees. And such practices have value in reminding us of the kind of attitude we should have when we pray. If we want to be close to God, we must put other activities out of our hands and minds and "kneel before the Lord our maker" (Psalm 95:6). Still, we can pray just as truly with our hands on the steering wheel and our eyes wide open, or in the hospital bed, flat on our backs, or with our hands in the dishwater. The only absolute requirement is that we talk with God.

TO SAY THANK YOU

The Christian has a lot to talk to God about, especially in the line of saying "Thank You." We thank our God for His loving plan of salvation and for including us in that plan. We thank our God for the church and the Bible and for Christian leaders and friends. We thank our God for life, for food and clothes, for the beauty in the world around us, and for God's "very present help in trouble" (Psalm 46:1).

God desires our thanks, too. Psalm 100:4 characterizes public worship this way: "Enter into his gates with thanksgiving, and into his courts with praise: be thankful unto him, and bless his name." The apostle Paul goes even further: "Give thanks in all circumstances; for this is the will of God in Christ Jesus for you" (I Thessalonians 5:18). The Heidelberg Catechism, written in 1563, spells out one of the main reasons for prayer when it says that "it is the chief part of the thankfulness which God requires of us . . . ".

A CRY FOR HELP

Prayer is also a cry for help. Doctors want new born babies to cry to show that they are alive. If the baby does not cry, the doctor shakes him or spanks him until he does. Otherwise he soon will be dead. For the same reason, God wants His children to cry to Him. "And because you are sons," says Paul, "God has sent the Spirit of his Son into our hearts, crying, 'Abba! Father!' " (Galatians 4:6). When they cry, God hears, "For he shall deliver the needy when he crieth; the poor also, and him that hath no helper" (Psalm 72:12).

What God's children should and may cry to Him about is contained in the compact yet complete prayer Jesus taught His disciples. "Pray then like this: 'Our Father who art in heaven, Hallowed be thy name. Thy kingdom come, Thy will be done, On earth as it is in heaven. Give us this day our daily bread; And forgive us our debts, As we also have forgiven our debtors; And lead us not into temptation, But deliver us from evil" (Matthew 6:9-13).

Because God is our Father by faith in Jesus, our first concern in prayer is about God Himself. We are concerned about the "hallowing" or making holy of His name. We are dedicated to that name, and are anxious to see that God receives the glory He deserves. We pray that His kingdom may come and may show itself in our hearts and conduct. We even pray that His will may be performed by us and by everyone all over the world — by presidents, mayors, students, teachers, parents, children, policemen, citizens.

We also are rightfully concerned about ourselves and those around us. So we pray for our daily bread. Not T-bone steaks, not great wealth, but bread. We pray for clothes and medicine and other necessities of life. "Feed me with the food that is needful for me" (Proverbs 30:8). And we come to God with our spiritual needs. God is well aware of our sins and wants us to be honest with Him about them. And when we confess our sins, God is happy to forgive them (see I John

1:8-10). Also in the matter of temptation, the best way to receive God's help is to ask for it.

PRAYER CHANGES THINGS

Does prayer really make a difference? Does it really change things, as a familiar little wall plaque says it does? If you have tried it and failed, perhaps it is because you did not pray that God's will be done. Perhaps "you ask and do not receive, because you ask wrongly" (James 4:3). Perhaps you failed because God could not give His blessing to what you asked for. Perhaps you simply haven't meant what you asked. Or perhaps you failed to ask in Jesus' name.

Prayer "works" only if it meets God's requirements. And the one requirement above all others is that our prayers be Christ-centered. In one of His great prayer lessons, Jesus said that "whatsoever ye shall ask in my name, that will I do, that the Father may be glorified in the Son. If ye shall ask anything in my name, I will do it" (John 14:13, 14). And He can make an amazing claim like that, "seeing he ever liveth to make intercession for them" (Hebrews 7:25).

When we pray in Jesus' name, which includes praying according to God's will, the guaranteed results are plain. "Ask, and it shall be given you; seek, and ye shall find; knock, and it shall be opened unto you" (Matthew 7:7). "Call unto me, and I will answer thee . . ." (Jeremiah 33:3). For "the effectual fervent prayer of a righteous man availeth much" (James 5:16).

So "pray without ceasing" (I Thessalonians 5:17). Pray with your family. Pray alone. Pray in church. Pray in the subway . . . at your work . . . when you are tempted . . . when you are happy . . . when you are sad. Tell God the things that are closest to your heart. Ask Him constantly to tune your will to His. For if you want spiritual victories, you will have to pray. Just as a soprano reaches that high note with a deep breath, and just as a runner gets that added spurt of energy through hard breathing, so the Christian reaches high and wins victories through constant and submissive prayer. His breath of life, your breath of life, is *prayer.*

QUESTIONS FOR FURTHER STUDY

1. Are long and fluent prayers better than short and simple ones? See Matthew 6:5-7; Luke 18:13, 14.
2. Read the parable of the Pharisee and the tax collector in Luke 18:9-14. The one prayer was acceptable to God, the other prayer was not. Why?
3. Paul said that we are to give thanks in all circumstances (I Thessalonians 5:18). Can we thank God for being sick, or for losing a dear one? See Job 1:21; Isaiah 55:9; Hebrews 12:7-11.
4. Did Jesus intend that we should memorize and recite the Lord's Prayer? Compare Matthew 6:9-13 with Luke 11:2-4.
5. What kind of "condition" does God attach to His forgiveness of the sins we confess to Him? See Matthew 6:13-15; 18:23-35.
6. Read Abraham's "intercessory prayer" in Genesis 18:22-33. What most impresses you about this prayer? Did God answer it? See Genesis 19:14-16.
7. If God does not seem to answer our prayers today, should we ask Him again tomorrow? See Luke 18:1-8.

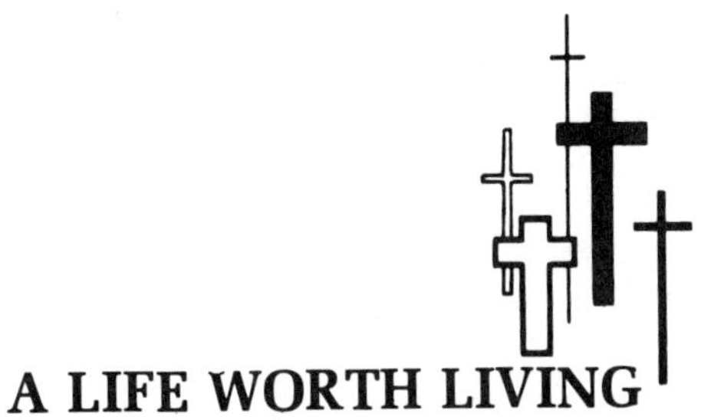

A LIFE WORTH LIVING

Somewhere on the island of Sumatra is a gravestone with the following inscription:

HERE REST THE BONES
OF THE TWO AMERICAN MISSIONARIES
MUNSON AND LYMAN
KILLED AND EATEN IN THE YEAR 1834
JOHN 16:1-3

These two men went as far as men can go in living up to Jesus' terms for discipleship in Mark 8:34, 35: "Whosoever will come after me, let him deny himself, and take up his cross, and follow me. For whosoever will save his life shall lose it; but whosoever shall lose his life for my sake and the gospel's, the same shall save it."

We can be thankful that not very many Christians lose their lives in the service of their Lord. In one way or another, however, every Christian must "deny himself" and "take up his cross." This may be only a small cross, such as breaking some bad habit or suffering ridicule for Christian convictions. Or it may mean a big cross, such as being rejected by your family and friends because of your Christian faith.

But whether these are large or small, we will have crosses. Jesus told His disciples, "If ye were of the world, the world would love his own; but because ye are not of the world, but I have chosen you out of the world, therefore the world hateth you" (John 15:19). And there must be self-denial. "Whosoever he be of you that forsaketh not all that he hath, he cannot be my disciple" (Luke 14:33).

A fair question to ask therefore is this: Is it worth it all? As Jesus Himself said, "For which of you, intending to build a tower, sitteth not down first, and counteth the cost, whether he have sufficient to finish it?" (Luke 14:28). In the light of such possible or actual cost, we repeat: Is the Christian life truly a life worth living?

IS IT WORTH IT FOR ME?

The Bible answers with a threefold Yes!

Yes, it is worth it for me. Consider these beautiful promises: "Whosoever therefore shall confess me before men, him will I also confess before my Father who is in heaven" (Matthew 10:32). Also, "The saying is sure: If we have died with him, we shall also live with him: if we endure, we shall also reign with him. . ." (II

Timothy 2:11, 12). "For we know that if the earthly tent we live in is destroyed, we have a building from God, a house not made with hands, eternal in the heavens" (II Corinthians 5:1).

Yes, the missionaries died, and the deaths they experienced were horrible. But their deaths introduced them to a glorious new life in the presence of their Lord. The same is true for all servants of Christ. So what if we have to give a little — suffer a little — endure a little? Christ has done as much and more for us. Besides, "This slight momentary affliction is preparing for us an eternal weight of glory beyond all comparison, because we look not to the things that are seen but to the things that are unseen. . . " (II Corinthians 4:17, 18).

Nor do we have to wait until we die to enjoy living for Christ. The moment Christ enters our lives, things change for the better. The testimony of Paul was not just that "to die is gain," but even before that: "For me to live is Christ" (Philippians 1:21). The Christian life is a daily joy, even if it involves crosses.

Sticking with it, then, even when the going is rough, is pretty good evidence that we are Christ's. If our faith is never tested, how can we be sure that it's real? On the other hand, when we are successfully fighting sin and are really going to work for Christ in our daily life, then we can say, "I by my works will show you my faith" (James 2:18). And as I convince you of my faith, I also convince myself.

IT IS WORTH IT FOR OTHERS

Living my life for God also has value for others. In the case of the two missionaries Munson and Lyman, they had worked among the Batak people for only one year when they met their death in 1834. And it was not until 1861, nearly thirty years later, that the first Batak Christian was baptized. Yet in 1922, less than eighty years after their death, there were 200,000 Batak Christians. What great blessings were brought to the Batak people — in part by the missionaries' living sacrifice! And what an inspiration their sacrifice is even to Christians

like ourselves, who tend to complain about much smaller sacrifices!

A dedicated Christian life is always of benefit to other Christians. When I go to church, not only do I refresh my faith; I also give a helpful example to my Christian neighbor who may have been tempted to stay home. When I refrain from swearing or telling dirty stories during the coffee break, I may be helping some other young Christian who is trying hard to improve his own habits. Christ expects us to have this concern for others, for in this way we encourage each other and build each other up. "We who are strong ought to bear with the failings of the weak, and not to please ourselves; let each of us please his neighbor for his good, to edify him" (Romans 15:1, 2).

A life lived for Christ can also be a great benefit to non-Christians. When I go about my work with a smile, "working heartily, as serving the Lord" (Colossians 3:23), this cannot but impress others who are watching me, and draw them toward the Lord whom I love and serve. When I take the time to visit a lonely widow or a sick child — when I share my money through offerings for the church and missions and related programs — when I tell of God and His love to my church school class or to my unchurched neighbor — when I demonstrate that love by helpfulness and kindness—not only am I enriching my faith and doing service to my Lord, I am also sharing my Christian happiness and my Christ with those whose lives are empty of His presence and peace.

IT IS WORTH IT FOR GOD

Finally, a Christian life is worth it from God's point of view. The Bible says again and again that God wants His children to live to His glory. "You are not your own; you were bought with a price. So glorify God in your body" (I Corinthians 6:19, 20). "But you are . . . God's own people, that you may declare the wonderful deeds of him who called you out of darkness into his marvelous light" (I Peter 2:9). "Whether therefore you eat, or drink, or whatsoever you do, do all to the glory of God" (I Corinthians 10:31).

First, by patterning our lives after God's law of

love, we serve God's glory. And second, by helping others along in their Christian living, and by leading others to faith by our example, those others join with us in bringing even greater glory to God. As Jesus says in Matthew 5:16, "Let your light so shine before men, that they may see your good works, and glorify your Father who is in heaven."

QUESTIONS FOR FURTHER STUDY

1. Jesus states the demands of the Christian life in Luke 9:57-62 and Luke 14:26, 33. How literally must we take these demands? See also Matthew 6:25, 33.
2. Have there been, or can there ever be, perfect Christians? See Job 1:1; Romans 3:23; I John 1:8; 3:9.
3. Philippians 3:12-14 makes plain that living for Christ is hard work. However, since nothing that we do will save us, and since even the best things we do are imperfect anyway, why must we still work so hard at Christian living? See Matthew 25:40; Romans 6:1, 2; 12:1, 2; I Corinthians 6:19, 20; Philippians 3:12b.
4. Evaluate the following statement in the light of Galatians 5:1: "As long as my conscience is clear, and as long as I am not breaking any of God's commandments, I can do whatever I please." See also Romans 14:13; 15:1, 2; Galatians 5:13.
5. Name some factors working against us as we try to live for God. See Romans 7:18; Ephesians 6:12; James 1:13, 14; I Peter 5:8.
6. What helps has God made available for our use in trying to live for Him? See Psalm 119:11; Matthew 26:41; Romans 8:26; Ephesians 6:10, 13-18; Hebrews 4:16.

JOINING THE CHRIST-GROUP

The title of a one-time very popular song is "Everybody Loves Somebody." Perhaps an even more true-to-life title would be "Everybody *wants to Be Loved* by Somebody." A child who has no friends is an unhappy child. A teen-ager who doesn't belong to some kind of group is "out of it." Even an adult who has no known relatives and no real friends is a sad and lonely person. Christians are no different from anyone else in this respect. They too want to be loved. They too want to belong.

Of course, anybody who is a Christian *is* loved—by God. And he *does* belong—to God through faith in Jesus Christ. And without a doubt his greatest happiness is in knowing that whether living or dying, he is Christ's and Christ is God's (I Corinthians 3:23).

CHRIST AND ME, PLUS

Yes, with a world full of people around us, and being social creatures as we are, any Christian who says that he is completely happy with just "Christ and me" and no one else is less than honest with himself. Let's face it, even for us as Christians, life can be pretty lonely if there is no one else with whom to share the experience of faith, and to whom we can belong. With the Christian it is not just "Christ and me." It is "Christ and me" — plus a whole lot of people "like me," people who also belong to Christ and who are a part of the Christ-group.

This Christ-group the Bible describes in many different ways. Most frequently it is called simply "the church" (Matthew 16:18; Acts 5:11; 11:26; I Corinthians 12:28; and others). Perhaps the best descriptive name given to the church is the one used many times by Paul: "Now you are the body of Christ and individually members of it" (I Corinthians 12:27).

THE BODY OF CHRIST

One thing this name brings out about the church is that the church has a head—Christ! Christ "is the head of the body, the church" (Colossians 1:18). "For the husband is the head of the wife as Christ is the head of the church, his body, and is himself its Savior" (Ephesians 5:23). Christ is the church's source of life and power. Christ is the brain center, nerve center, and command center. Therefore, in any church that is truly Christian, the Word of Christ is the last word.

Another point about the body of Christ is that each member of that body has to be connected to Christ. Since Christ's church is "the church of God, which he has purchased with his own blood" (Acts 20:28), that church includes only those who are individually members of it by saving faith in His shed blood. No one is ever a member of Christ's body simply because of the color of his skin, or his family history, or his community position.

A third point is that all those who are a part of Christ's body are also part of one another. "So we, though many, are one body in Christ, and individually members one of another" (Romans 12:5). It's something like one Christian being the right hand, another being the left hand; one Christian being the right foot, another being the left foot. Obviously it does no good to have two hands or two feet unless those hands and feet cooperate. This same kind of harmony characterizes the church of Christ. "God has so adjusted the body . . . that there may be no discord in the body but that the members may have the same care for one another. If one member suffers, all suffer together; if one member is honored, all rejoice together" (I Corinthians 12:24-26). This wonderful fact of belonging is called "the communion of saints" (Apostles' Creed).

AN INVISIBLE BODY

How can I join the Christ-group so that I too belong?

If you are a Christian, you already belong. For in the sense that the body of Christ consists of

that great company of people "from every tribe and tongue and people and nation" who belong to Christ, including those living on earth as well as those living in heaven, and including Brethren, Episcopalians, Methodists, Lutherans, Presbyterians, Roman Catholics, Reformed, and the like — in that sense any Christian is a member of the body of Christ. If you are a member of Christ by faith, you are a member of the one "holy catholic church" (Apostles' Creed).

VISIBLE BODIES OF CHRIST

The body of Christ also takes shape in another way — in organized churches or congregations, neighborhood Christ-groups. A number of like-minded Christ-groups are called "denominations." Thinking of the church in this sense, church membership is not automatic. To belong to some visible body of Christ, you have to join it.

This kind of membership is also important. For how strange if someone who is a member of the invisible body of Christ does not want to be a member of some visible evidence of the body of Christ! A Christian who chooses not to join some visible Christ-group is something like a drummer without a band, or like or soldier without an army.

Joining some visible part of the body of Christ is important for two reasons. The first reason is that church membership is a means by which we confess our faith in Christ. When you confess before God and a congregation of Christians that you are Christ's and want to live for Him, not only are you entitled to membership in that church, but in the eyes of the world you have set yourself apart as a Christian. "For a man believes with his heart and so is justified, and he confesses with his lips and so is saved" (Romans 10:10).

The second reason why joining some visible part of the body of Christ is important is that church membership opens the door to all the helps the church offers for the constant spiritual improvement of its members. As a member, not only do you benefit from the preaching and study of the Bible, friendship, and prayer for each other, but full membership in the church of Christ entitles you to the sacraments of baptism and the Lord's Supper. Both of these sacraments are most important to the diet of active and growing Christians. What's more, as a confessing member of the "flock of God" you come under the loving supervision of church leaders whose responsibility it is to "tend the flock of God that is [their] charge" (I Peter 5:2).

THE CHURCH OF YOUR CHOICE

Because of the many churches in every community that claim to be Christian, one tremendously important question remains: Which church or congregation should I join? Basically, the things to look for in the church of your choice are the three things pointed out earlier about the body of Christ: (1) Is Christ the true head of this church? Does this church hold fast the word of life (Philippians 2:16), and does it "hold to the traditions" (II Thessalonians 2:15) of the historic Christian church? In other words, does this church preach the true Word of God? Does this church administer the sacraments according to the clear commands of Christ? (2) Is it plain that its members are members of Christ? Are they Christ-like in their attitudes and actions? Do they bear fruit? (See John 15:4.) Do they follow Christ's voice? (See John 10:4.) Involved in these questions is the matter of what is commonly called church discipline. When a church has members who confess to belong to Christ, and yet deny Christ in the way they live, does the church discipline those members? And

if those members refuse to repent of their sinfulness, does this church care enough about the purity of the body of Christ to exclude them from its membership? After all, a Christian church has no business accepting into its membership, or retaining in its membership, those who prove by their conduct that they are not really living parts of the body of Christ. (3) Does this church offer real communion of the saints? Do they welcome into their fellowship all who want to worship and work for Christ, regardless of race, or social standing, or national origin? In other words, do the members of this church love one another?

If this is a picture of the church of your choice, or if it is as close to this picture as you can find, by all means join it. For by so doing, you will be better able in God's grace to "grow up into him in all things, who is the head, even Christ" (Ephesians 4:15).

If the church of your choice meets these requirements, you should receive much added happiness as a member of it.

QUESTIONS FOR FURTHER STUDY

1. Make a list of the different ways in which the Bible uses the word "church." See Matthew 16:18; Act 5:11; 11:26; 14:23; I Corinthians 14:23; Ephesians 1:22; Revelation 22:16. (It may also be helpful to consult a book on Christian doctrine.)
2. How do we understand the statement from the Apostles' Creed, "I believe a holy *catholic* Church"? See Revelation 5:9. Should we use a different word here than "catholic"? Give reasons for your answer.
3. What kind of people are eligible for church membership? See Acts 2:39, 47; 17:26; Galatians 3:28; Revelation 5:9.
4. Is it fitting to address other Christians as "brothers" and "sisters"? See Romans 12:4, 5; Ephesians 4:4-6.
5. Discuss the following: "Not every church member is a member of the Christian church." See Matthew 7:21; Romans 9:6b; I Corinthians 5:13.
6. What is the meaning of the expression "keys of the kingdom" as found in Matthew 16:19?

CHAPTER 21

YOU AND YOUR FAMILY

Hundreds of years ago people were sometimes branded so that others would know what kind of people they were. The Greeks branded their slaves with a large letter "D" (for *doulos*). Robbers were branded by the Romans with the letter "F" (for *fugitives*). The ancient laws of England approved the branding of certain people, such as runaway slaves or army deserters, often on the cheek or forehead.

THE BRAND OF BAPTISM

When someone joins a Christian church he certainly is not branded with a capital letter. Yet the Christian is given a kind of brand or mark of ownership to designate that he belongs to God by faith in Christ. That brand or mark performed on the Christian is the sacrament of Christian baptism.

Baptism is not a brand in the sense of leaving a scar or mark. In fact, baptism is nothing more than a simple ceremony in which a Christian minister sprinkles or pours water on a person's head (or in some churches places him completely into the water). A person is baptized into the name of our Triune God: Father, Son, and Holy Spirit. But as simple and as painless as this ceremony is, Jesus clearly commanded that all new Christians shall be baptized. "Go ye therefore, and make disciples of all the nations, baptizing them into the name of the Father and of the Son and of the Holy Spirit" (Matthew 28:19).

GOD DRAWS A PICTURE

Water is used for washing — our bodies, our clothes, our homes, and even our streets. Baptism, then, is God's way of drawing a picture of our spiritual washing. We learn from John 3:25, 26 that the baptism of John the Baptist was related to the Jewish ceremony of "purification." This same idea is at the center of Christian baptism. Hebrews 10:22 describes Christian salvation as having "our hearts sprinkled clean from an evil conscience and our bodies washed with pure water." Peter writes of baptism "not as a removal of dirt from the body but as an appeal to God for a clear conscience" (I Peter 3:21). Paul was told the same thing at the time of his baptism: "Arise, and be baptized, and wash away your sins, calling on the name of the Lord" (Acts 22:16). Water does to the body what the blood of Jesus does to the Christian's soul.

GOD MAKES A PROMISE

With the drawing of this picture in baptism, God also makes a promise. He is saying to the Christian, "As surely as water washes dirt from the body, the blood of Jesus washes away your sins." Baptism helps us to remember and believe that God the Son has earned the forgiveness of our sins, that God the Father has adopted us as His children, and that God the Holy Spirit lives in our hearts. In the sight of God our record is clean, and so are our souls. This water is our proof! our receipt! our guarantee!

But this is not to say that the water of baptism itself does the cleansing. If that were the case, all that the Christian church would have to do is gather up an army, force baptism upon everyone at the point of a bayonet, and it would have saved the entire human race. Water, all by itself, washes only the outside of the body — even the water in baptism. Baptism has no magic power. Baptism gives me nothing I did not have before. For this reason, too, the amount of water used in baptism makes no difference. Baptism pictures and promises absolutely nothing if the person baptized rejects God's promises.

A person's right to membership in a visible Christian church depends not upon his baptism, but upon faith. Baptism has value only in relation to one's faith. Baptism pictures and promises to the Christian only *what he already has* by faith in God's Word and work. For that reason, "He who believes and is baptized shall be saved; he who does not believe shall be condemned" (Mark 16:16).

YOU AND YOUR FAMILY

Most of what has been said thus far applies mainly to those who come to know and accept Christ as adults. In the early New Testament church most of the people who were baptized were adults. To them, the news that Jesus is the Christ was truly *news*. All Christians were necessarily *new* Christians. Since there could be no adults who had been Christians from an early age, all adults were baptized as adults.

Yet God's promise of salvation in Christ was not theirs only, but theirs *and their children's*. In the words of Peter, "For the promise is to you and to your children. . . " (Acts 2:39). The promise that God had made long before this to Abraham — "I will establish my covenant between me and thee and thy seed after thee in their generations for an everlasting covenant, to be a God unto thee, and to thy seed after thee" (Genesis 17:7) — is a promise that is true for all generations. For "if you are Christ's, then you are Abraham's offspring, heirs according to promise" (Galatians 3:29). Therefore as Paul told the Philippian jailor, "Believe on the Lord Jesus and you will be saved, you and your family" (Acts 16:31).

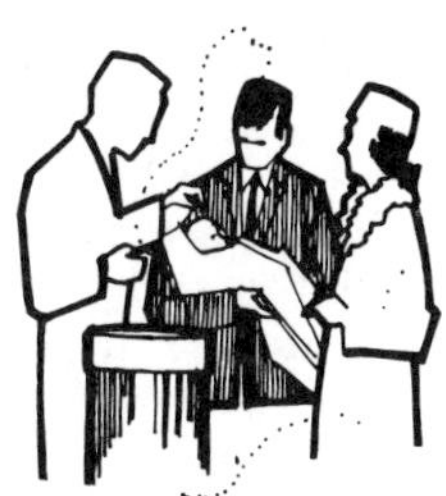

Just as the promise is given to the children, so also the sacrament should be given to the children. In the Old Testament, God commanded that circumcision be performed not only on the adult males who shared God's promises, but on male infants also, and even on the male servants. Therefore, since baptism has taken the place of circumcision as God's mark of ownership (see Colossians 2:11, 12), it is only natural that the children of believers should be baptized.

So when Paul and Silas told the Philippian jailor that God saved in a family way, and when the jailor believed, "he was baptized at once with all his family" (Acts 16:33). "I baptized also the household of Stephanas" (I Corinthians 1:16), writes Paul. Lydia too "was baptized, and her household" (Acts 16:15).

PARENTAL RESPONSIBILITY

To this wonderful "you and your family" promise, God adds a heavy responsibility. God made the "covenant" or arrangement with Abraham that He would be his God and the God of his children as long as Abraham and his children agreed to be His people (see Genesis 17:1, 7, 9). This same arrangement continues in the New Testament. The clear duty of Christian parents toward their children is to "bring them up

in the nurture and admonition of the Lord"
(Ephesians 6:4).

The church is ready and eager to help Christian parents in this task. And in many areas parents can send their child to a Christian school as a further help. But even with both of these helps on hand to assist them in the Christian training of their child, the parents still have the basic responsibility for their child's soul. God says to every believing parent, "And these words, which I command thee this day, shall be in thine heart; and thou shalt teach them diligently unto thy children, and thou shalt talk of them when thou sittest in thy house, and when thou walkest by the way, and when thou liest down, and when thou risest up" (Deuteronomy 6:6, 7).

QUESTIONS FOR FURTHER STUDY

1. Nowhere does the New Testament command "by immersion only." Is it likely that all early Christian baptisms were by immersion? See Acts 2:4; 9:18; 10:47; 16:33, 34.
2. In what way was the baptism of Jesus different from the baptism of Christians? See Matthew 3:13-17; John 1:29-34.
3. The main basis for infant baptism is the "covenant of grace," as stated in Genesis 17:1-7 and repeated in Acts 2:39 and elsewhere. Name the agreeing parties, the promise, and the conditions in this covenant.
4. The above-mentioned Scripture passages promise God's saving grace to believers and to their children. Does this promise also apply to adopted children? See Romans 9:8.
5. May an infant be baptized if only one of his parents is a confessing Christian? See I Corinthians 7:14.

CHAPTER 22

TO HELP YOU GROW UP

The birth of a healthy baby is a happy event in a home. Announcements are made; candy and cigars may be passed out; gifts and congratulations are received. But the birth of the baby is by no means the end of the story. The baby must be fed and changed; he must have rest; he must get shots; he must be coddled and clothed and cared for until he is grown-up.

The same thing is true with Christians. The responsibility for our new life does not end when we are born again. God's goal for those who belong to Christ is that they "all attain to the unity of the faith and of the knowledge of the Son of God, to mature manhood, to the measure of the stature of the fulness of Christ; so that we may no longer be children. . . . Rather, speaking the truth in love, we are to grow up in every way

into him who is the head, into Christ. . ."
(Ephesians 4:13-15).

TO HELP YOU GROW UP

Just as milk, love, food, and care are needed to help a baby grow up, so the "growing combination" for young Christians is "the apostles' doctrine and fellowship, the breaking of bread and the prayers" (Acts 2:42).

The apostles' doctrine or teaching is given to us in the Bible. Peter compared the Bible to a baby's milk: "Like newborn babes, long for the pure spiritual milk, that by it you may grow up to salvation" (I Peter 2:2). Constant "eating and drinking" of the Bible is as necessary to a Christian's health as milk is to a baby. If you neglect the Sunday sermons, or the Bible study classes, or your own personal Bible reading, the only result can be an "undernourished" Christian. You cannot overcome temptation, enjoy your faith, or expect to live victoriously in a weakened spiritual condition.

Take advantage, too, of the "fellowship" your church offers. Every meeting of Christians —worship services, society meetings, church picnics —is a kind of pep-rally. For this reason the Bible tells us, "And let us consider how to stir up one another to love and good works, not neglecting to meet together, as is the habit of some, but encouraging one another, and all the more as you see the Day drawing near" (Hebrews 10:24, 25). Just as a baby needs the love and encouragement of his parents and family, so Christians need the love and encouragement of other Christians to perform well for their Lord.

A third item on the church's menu for growing Christians is "the prayers." Jesus said,

"Abide in me, and I in you. As the branch cannot bear fruit of itself, except it abide in the vine; no more can you, except you abide in me" (John 15:4). Abiding in Christ through regular prayer is absolutely necessary to a healthy and productive Christian life. (Also see Chapter 18.)

THE BREAKING OF BREAD 

The church's menu for growing Christians also includes what is known in Acts 2:42 as "the breaking of bread." Today it usually is called the "Lord's Supper" or "Holy Communion." This is the second of the two sacraments Jesus commanded to be used by the Christian church.

Jesus initiated the Lord's Supper the night before His death, during His last Passover meal with His disciples. The Passover meal was a custom that had begun when the Israelites were freed from Egyptian slavery, about thirteen centuries before Jesus's time. On that memorable night of the first Passover, the angel of death had slain the oldest child in every Egyptian home, but had "passed over" the homes of the Israelites because they had sprinkled the blood of a lamb on their doorframes, as God had commanded. The blood of the lamb was only a symbol, of course, of the blood of Christ who saves us from our sins by His death.

So on the night before Jesus' saving death, "the Lamb of God" (John 1:29) gave a new meaning and form to the ancient Passover meal. Matthew recalls that "as they were eating, Jesus took bread, and blessed, and broke it, and gave it to the disciples and said, 'Take, eat; this is my body.' And he took a cup, and when he had given thanks he gave it to them, saying, 'Drink of it, all of you: for this is my blood of the covenant, which is poured out for many for the forgiveness of sins' '' (Matthew 26:26-28).

Ever since that time the Lord's Supper has become an important item on the menu for healthy and growing Christians. The reasons are obvious.

First, our Lord commanded that His followers "do this in remembrance of me" (I Corinthians 11:24, 26). Second, the Lord's Supper is God's way of picturing and promising nourishment and spiritual energy for the new life. This nourishment is received by faith in Christ and His saving work. As Paul explained, "The cup of blessing which we bless, is it not a participation in the blood of Christ? The bread which we break, is it not a participation in the body of Christ?" (I Corinthians 10:16). The bread and the cup are symbols or pictures of the body and blood of Christ, and the eating and drinking are symbols of receiving Christ and His saving work by faith.

Third, the Lord's Supper is a kind of divine guarantee that reassures and builds up our faith. Christ is truly present by His Spirit in the Communion service to bless us; and through the symbols of the bread and wine He provides a renewed fellowship with Himself, who is the true food and drink of life eternal.

The idea of the Lord's Supper, then, is that just as eating and drinking gives renewed life and strength to our bodies, so eating "the bread which we break" and drinking "the cup of blessing" — *by faith* in the broken body and poured-out blood of Christ — gives renewed life to our souls.

LET A MAN EXAMINE HIMSELF

In the celebration of the Lord's Supper, the two all-important words are "by faith." We are to remember *and believe* that Christ's body and blood were offered up for the forgiveness of our sins. If we have no faith in this message of the Lord's Supper, it accomplishes absolutely nothing and has no more spiritual effect upon us than having a coffee break or eating a cracker. In fact, to partake of the Supper without understanding what it is all about, or without having faith in its meaning, is worse than not partaking at all: "Whoever, therefore, eats the bread or drinks the cup of the Lord in an unworthy manner will be guilty of profaning the body and blood of the Lord. For any one who eats and drinks without discerning the body eats and drinks judgment upon himself" (I Corinthians 11:27, 29).

Therefore, "Let a man examine himself, and so eat of the bread and drink of the cup" (I Corinthians 11:28). Only when you have repentance in your heart for your sins can the Supper picture and promise to you the forgiveness of your sins through the broken body and shed blood of Christ. Only when you have true faith in the Savior can the Supper feed that faith. Only when you already desire to make improvements in your Christian life can the Supper strengthen that desire to live for God.

But when you put yourself to this threefold test and can give yourself a passing mark (not because you are so good, but because your repentance and faith and desire to live for God are real), then you can partake of the Lord's Supper and celebrate it in confidence. And you will find that your partaking of it will help you to grow up into Christ and will help you along the road of victorious Christian living. Jesus' own words are, "For my flesh is food indeed, and my blood is drink indeed. He who eats my flesh and drinks my blood abides in me, and I in him" (John 6:55, 56), and "Blessed are they which do hunger and thirst after righteousness: for they shall be filled" (Matthew 5:6). To be "blessed" and "filled" is to be happy.

QUESTIONS FOR FURTHER STUDY

1. Do church members always "grow"? If not, why not? See Matthew 13:18-23; I Timothy 4:10; Hebrews 5:11-14.
2. Some churches have as many as seven sacraments. Why do most Protestant churches have only two? See Matthew 28:19; I Corinthians 11:23-26.
3. Read the story of the Passover in Exodus 11; 12:1-28. In what way is the Lord's Supper similar to this feast? In what way is the Lord's Supper different?
4. Jesus said of the bread, "This is my body," and of the wine, "This is my blood." See Matthew 26:26-28. How are we to understand these statements? Do we actually eat the body and drink the blood of Christ?
5. Paul teaches us that "self-examination" is very important to a right celebration of the Lord's Supper. See I Corinthians 11:27-32. In what way does your church help you to prepare and celebrate the Lord's Supper properly? Can a child "examine himself"? an unbeliever?
6. Do church leaders ever have a right to ask individuals not to partake of the Lord's Supper? See Matthew 16:19; I Corinthians 5:11; I Peter 5:2, 3.

CHAPTER 23

PARTNERS IN A BIG BUSINESS

The Christian church in the world owns land, erects buildings, publishes and distributes literature, purchases radio and television time, owns and operates schools and hospitals, and invests millions of dollars each year in its program and work at home and in its missions all over the world.

The Christian church is a big business because it has the big commission of Jesus. "All authority in heaven and on earth has been given to me. Go therefore and make disciples of all nations, baptizing them in the name of the Father and of the Son and of the Holy Spirit, teaching them to observe all that I have commanded you" (Matthew 28:18-20). These parting words of Jesus to His disciples suggest the big business of His church in the world.

THE BIG BUSINESS OF THE CHURCH

The church must "go and make disciples" by preaching the good news of God's love in Christ Jesus. It must point the world to Christ who said,

"I am the way, the truth, and the life; no man comes to the Father, but by me" (John 14:6). In cathedrals and churches, in adobe huts and backwoods cabins, by radio and television and printed page it must "preach the word, be urgent in season and out of season, convince, rebuke, and exhort. . . " (II Timothy 4:2).

Second, it is the business of the church to offer the sacraments. All who become disciples of Jesus, and their children, must be baptized. The followers of Christ are also to "proclaim the Lord's death until he comes" (I Corinthians 11:26) in the celebration of the Lord's Supper, under the supervision of the church, which in turn is guided by the Bible.

Third, Christ commanded His church to be in the business of "teaching them to observe all that I have commanded you" (Matthew 28:20). This includes the twofold program of feeding the "sheep" and the "lambs" of the church (see John 21:15,17). Through the Sunday sermons, societies, church schools, home studies, and the like, the church must help its members to apply the Word of God to all areas of life. On behalf of the children and youth of the church, it must provide instruction in the teachings of the Bible through such means as Sunday school, doctrine classes, vacation Bible schools, Bible clubs, and by giving support where possible to Christian day schools and Christian schools of higher learning.

The business of the church is also service. Jesus prayed to His father, "As thou hast sent me into the world, even so have I also sent them into the world" (John 17:18). After the example of the Good Samaritan, Christians are to show mercy (see Luke 10:37), even to their enemies (see Matthew 5:38-48). James wrote, "Religion that is pure and undefiled before God and the

Father is this: to visit orphans and widows in their affliction, and to keep oneself unstained from the world" (James 1:27). And Paul commanded, "Always seek to do good to one another and to all" (I Thessalonians 5:15). Slum conditions, racial discrimination, the sick, the homeless, the hungry, the world's poor—all are the business of the Christian church.

THE BOARD OF DIRECTORS

In the running of any large business, not even ten people—let alone thousands and thousands of people—can operate smoothly unless some have the responsibility of leadership and the others are willing to follow their lead. So it is also in the Christian church. The head of the church is Christ (see Chapter 20). He is the "chairman of the board." His Word is always the last word. However, He did appoint a kind of "board of directors" to direct the church under His Lordship, and He even sent the Holy Spirit to guide them in directing the church in its business (see John 14:26; Acts 1:8). This board of directors was the twelve apostles. They were hand-picked by Jesus Himself (with the exception of Matthias, Acts 1:26), they had been with Jesus from the time of His baptism, and they were witnesses of His resurrection (see Acts 1:21-25). On the basis of their confession that Jesus is "the Christ, the Son of the living God," Jesus gave to them "the keys of the kingdom of heaven" (see Matthew 16:16-19) to lead and direct His church.

Since there would be no Christians in future generations who would meet the qualifications of "apostles," and with the church growing as it was, the apostles themselves began to establish new offices. Already in Acts 6 the apostles initiated the office of deacon. The deacons were to care for the poor and help generally in the work of the church. And in Acts 14:23 we learn that "they had appointed elders for them in every church." To the elders was given the important task of "caring for God's church" (I Timothy 3:5) as teachers and as rulers. In addition, the apostles and the elders—with the approval of the churches—sent out missionaries (see Acts 15:22), and the office of pastors and teachers was also established (see Ephesians 4:11). Today it is through the offices that Christ directs and accomplishes the business of His church.

Although these leaders usually are chosen by the congregations themselves, they are responsible to Christ and His Word—not for their own glory, but for His service (see Matthew 20:24-28; John 13:12-17). The task of the elders and pastors is to direct the church's business of preaching, baptizing, and teaching. They are to see to it that "all things should be done decently and in order" (I Corinthians 14:40). And they have the special responsibility of caring for the spiritual lives of the church's members. They are to "admonish the idle, encourage the faint-hearted, help the weak, be patient with them all" (I Thessalonians 5:14). And for the honor of Christ and the purity of the church, they must exercise Christian discipline wherever necessary (see Matthew 18:17; I Corinthians 5:9-13).

PARTNERS IN A BIG BUSINESS

The biggest possible mistake, however, would be to think that only the church leaders are to be interested and involved in the business of the church. For every individual Christian, church membership is a privilege *and* a responsibility. Just as every Christian is a member of Christ's body, so every Christian is a partner in the church's business.

Each and every Christian is duty bound to share his knowledge of Christ with others through personal witnessing and daily conduct (see Matthew 5:14-16; Acts 1:8; Galatians 6:6; Philippians 2:14-16; I Peter 2:9; 3:15). Every Christian is expected to be a "financial partner" in the program of the local church, the care of the poor, and the support of mission work (see Proverbs 19:17; Mark 12:41-44; I Corinthians 16:1, 2; II Corinthians 8:1-5; 9:6-15; Galatians 2:10; Ephesians 4:28; Philippians 4:14-18). All Christians are partners in the important ministry of prayer for the business of the church (see Matthew 9:28; Acts 12:12; Romans 15:30; Ephesians 6:18, 19; I Thessalonians 5:17, 25; James 5:16). All Christians are responsible for the spiritual well-being of their fellow Christians (see Matthew 18:15, 16; Romans 15:1, 2; Galatians 6:1, 2). All Christians share responsibility for the peace and harmony of the church (see John 13:34, 35; Romans 12:16; Galatians 5:26). And all Christians are partners in Christian service (see Matthew 5:38-42; Romans 12:21; Galatians 6:9). Just as one irresponsible salesman can ruin the name of the whole company, so any one Christian who fails in his partnership responsibility causes loss to the whole church of Christ.

Therefore, "having gifts that differ according to the grace given to us, let us use them: if prophecy, in proportion to our faith; if service, in our serving; he who teaches, in his teaching; he who exhorts, in his exhortation; he who contributes, in liberality; he who gives aid, with zeal; he who does acts of mercy, with cheerfulness" (Romans 12:6-8). Such living enables you to say, "For to me to live is Christ, and to die is gain" (Philippians 1:21). And that is real happiness!

QUESTIONS FOR FURTHER STUDY

1. In view of the qualifications for an apostle listed in Acts 1:21-25, does Paul have the right to call himself an apostle? See I Corinthians 15:8-10; Galatians 1:1, 11-17.
2. The Roman Catholic Church claims to be the only true church because the pope is leader in an unbroken line from Peter (the alleged first pope). See Matthew 16:16-18. Does "this rock" that Jesus here mentions refer to Peter or to his confession? The Mormons claim to have the true church because it has twelve apostles. What gives a church the right to be called a Christian church?
3. What personal qualifications does the Bible demand of those who serve as elders (also called bishops) or deacons? See Acts 6:1-6; I Timothy 3:1-13; Titus 1:5-9.
4. Make a personal list of the ways in which you can be a partner in the church's program of worship, education, service, fellowship, and witness to the community and to the world. Perhaps your pastor can offer more suggestions.
5. Should a Christian "tithe"? See Numbers 18:21-32. How much should a Christian give? See I Corinthians 16:2; II Corinthians 8:3; 9:6, 7. Also see Matthew 19:21; Mark 12:41-44.
6. All Christians do not have the same abilities and gifts. How then does God judge our Christian service? See Matthew 25:14-30; Roman 12:6.